Walden

Volatile Truths

Twayne's Masterwork Studies

Robert Lecker, General Editor

Walden

Volatile Truths

Martin Bickman

Twayne Publishers • New York
Maxwell Macmillan Canada • Toronto
Maxwell Macmillan International • New York Oxford Singapore Sydney

Twayne's Masterwork Studies
No. 91

Walden: Volatile Truths
Martin Bickman

Twayne Publishers
Macmillan Publishing Company
866 Third Avenue
New York, New York 10022

Maxwell Macmillan Canada, Inc.
1200 Eglinton Avenue East
Suite 200
Don Mills, Ontario M3C 3N1

Macmillan Publishing Company is part of the
Maxwell Communication Group of Companies.

Library of Congress Cataloging-in-Publication Data

Bickman, Martin, 1945–
    Walden : volatile truths / Martin Bickman.
    p.   cm. — (Twayne's masterworks studies : 91)
    Includes bibliographical references and index.
    ISBN 0-8057-7958-2 — ISBN 0-8057-8012-2 (pbk.)
    1. Thoreau, Henry David, 1817–1862.   Walden.
                    I. Title.
    II. Series: Twayne's masterwork studies; no. 91.
                PS3048.B5   1992
818'.303—dc20   92-1187
                                           CIP

The paper used in this publication meets the mini-
mum requirements of American National Standard
for Information Sciences—Permanence of Paper for
Printed Library Materials. ANSI Z3948-1984. ∞ ™

10 9 8 7 6 5 4 3 2 1 (hc)
10 9 8 7 6 5 4 3 2 1 (pb)

Printed in the United States of America

For Louise

There is no remedy for love but to love more.
—Henry David Thoreau,
Journal, 25 July 1839

Contents

Henry David Thoreau

Woodcut by Antonio Frasconi, from "A Vision of Thoreau," 1965, permission by the artist

Note on the References and Acknowledgments

Fortunately, the text of *Walden* used by most critics and scholars—the one edited by J. Lyndon Shanley and published by Princeton University Press in 1971—is now available in a paperback edition for the general reader (Princeton, N.J.: Princeton University Press, 1989; foreword by Joyce Carol Oates). Formerly this text was available as a paperback only in the more expensive *The Illustrated "Walden*," also published by Princeton (1973). All three editions reproduce the same plates, and so the pagination used in parentheses in this volume applies to all of them. The new edition of Thoreau's *Journal*, also by Princeton University Press, is in the process of publication, but only the first three volumes have appeared. Because these volumes offer a more accurate and complete text, I have used them where possible. They are cited parenthetically in the text in arabic numerals, followed by page number, as in (2:17), while the older Houghton Mifflin edition (1906) is cited in roman numerals, followed by page number, as in (XI:26).

Walden, whatever else it is, is a heavily allusive book. I have not tried to gloss all the literary and historic references a modern reader might need to have explained, both because this task would take up most of the present volume and because it has been done well already—twice, in fact—by Walter Harding in *The Variorum "Walden"* (New York: Twayne, 1962) and Philip Van Doren Stern in *The Annotated "Walden"* (New York: Clarkson N. Potter, 1970).

During the writing of this book, I had the opportunity to observe *Walden* being taught in a laboratory course I supervise, "Teaching Literature," wherein graduate students instruct an undergraduate class together and analyze this class in terms of literary and educational theory. I thank both graduate and undergraduate groups for teaching me a great deal about reading this book and for their intelligence and goodwill.

I am grateful also to Heidi Olinger, my research assistant on this project, for her diligence, resourcefulness, and good humor.

I wish to thank my children, Sarah and Jed, for their general exuberant stance toward life and for their patience on drizzly hikes around Walden Pond.

As usual, my greatest debt is recorded in the dedication.

Chronology: Henry David Thoreau's Life and Works

1817   Born 12 July on maternal grandmother's farm on Virginia Road in Concord, Massachusetts, to John and Cynthia (Dunbar) Thoreau as the third of four children. Baptized 12 October as David Henry Thoreau by Dr. Ezra Ripley.

1818   Family moves first from the farm to Concord village, then to Chelmsford, 10 miles north, where father struggles as a grocer. Often stays awake at night "looking through the stars to see if I could see God behind them."

1821   Father is forced to close unsuccessful shop in Chelmsford and moves family to Boston, where he teaches and where Henry himself starts school.

1822   Taken on a family outing from Boston to Concord and sees Walden Pond for the first time.

1823   Family settles back in Concord. Henry attends private "infant school" and the public Center School, at which he will later teach for two weeks. Father begins pencil-making business, and mother takes in boarders.

1827   Writes first known essay, "The Seasons," for a school assignment.

1828   Enrolls with brother John in Concord Academy.

1833   Family has resources to send only one son to college. Henry enters Harvard, while siblings John and Helen teach school.

1835   Between terms, teaches school in Canton, Massachusetts, where he boards and studies German with a young minister, Orestes Brownson, who will soon publish key transcendentalist tract, *New Views of Christianity, Society, and the Church.*

1837   Reads Ralph Waldo Emerson's *Nature* while a senior at Harvard, from which he graduates on 30 August. This summer he also visits Charles Stearns Wheeler, his Harvard roommate during freshman year, living in a hut near Flint's Pond. After graduation, returns to

Concord to take a teaching position at the Center School; leaves after two weeks in a dispute over flogging students, later claiming that he viewed "cowhide as a nonconductor."

1838   Delivers first lecture, on "Society," before the Concord Lyceum. After searching for other teaching positions, opens own school in family home and then is able to take over the Concord Academy.

1839   Enough students enroll so that brother John joins as a teacher. Both brothers fall in love with Ellen Sewall, sister of one of their students, who visits Concord this summer.

1840   First literary publications, poem "Sympathy" and essay "Aulis Persius Flaccus," in the inaugural issue of the *Dial*, transcendentalist journal first edited by Margaret Fuller. Ellen Sewall rejects first John, then Henry as suitors.

1841   School closes because of John's tuberculosis. Turns down invitation to join Brook Farm, transcendentalist commune, but moves into Emerson household as handyman and gardener, where he stays until 1843.

1842   John, after cutting his finger on a razor, contracts lockjaw and dies, 11 January, in his brother's arms. Henry contracts a psychosomatic illness with symptoms of lockjaw, from which it takes him a month to recover. With Emerson's encouragement, writes for the *Dial* "Natural History of Massachusetts," in which he first starts to find his own voice and subject matter.

1843   Guest editor for April *Dial*. In May goes to live at the Staten Island home of William Emerson, Waldo's brother, to tutor William's three sons, but also with the hope of making contacts in literary and publishing circles. Meets Henry James, Sr., Horace Greeley, and Albert Brisbane but publishes only an essay, "The Landlord," and a book review, "Paradise (To Be) Regained," in *Democratic Review*. Also publishes "A Winter Walk" in *Dial* and "A Walk to Wachusett" in the *Boston Miscellany*. After six months, homesickness gets the best of him, and he returns to Concord in December.

1844   Living with his family and working in his father's pencil factory, he devises better production methods to create an award-winning pencil. January *Dial* publishes his translations from Pindar. In April, on a fishing trip with Edward Hoar, he negligently sets a fire that would burn more than 300 hundred wooded acres. Incurs Concord's anger and may have been prosecuted had his young companion not been the son of the town's leading citizen. Gets experience in building as he and his father construct the "Texas House" for the family.

1845   In late March begins cutting down pine trees with a borrowed ax on the shores of Walden Pond, on land owned by Emerson. Moves into still-unfinished cabin 4 July. Begins drafting first book, *A Week on the Concord and Merrimack Rivers*, and begins extensive journal entries about life in the woods that would become part of *Walden*.

1846 In February he lectures on Thomas Carlyle at the Concord Lyceum, where he says some of his audience hoped and expected to hear instead about his life at the pond. On 23 or 24 July is imprisoned for not paying his poll tax. Is released from jail against his will the next morning, after someone—probably an aunt—pays the tax for him. In August makes his first trip through the Maine Woods, ascending Mount Kaatdn.

1847 Gives two lectures on his life at Walden from material that now takes up the "Economy" chapter. The Carlyle lecture appears as an article in *Graham's Magazine*, March and April issues, placed there with the help of Horace Greeley. Leaves Walden Pond on 6 September to help run the Emerson household while Waldo makes an extended European trip.

1848 In January gives two lectures, each based on summer experiences of Walden Pond period, his trip to Kaatdn, and his arrest and one-night imprisonment for not paying poll tax. The first becomes the basis for a long, serialized piece in *Sartain's Union Magazine* and for the first part of the posthumously published *The Maine Woods*; the second for his most famous essay, which came to be known as "Civil Disobedience." Begins long correspondence with his chief disciple and future literary executor, Harrison Gray Otis Blake of Worcester.

1849 Second 1848 lecture published as "Resistance to Civil Liberty" in the first and only issue of Elizabeth Peabody's *Aesthetic Papers*. First trip to Cape Cod. *A Week on the Concord and Merrimack Rivers* published 28 October by James Munroe. Of 1,000 copies printed, 219 are sold, 75 given away.

1850 Busy as a surveyor. On second visit to Cape Cod, takes steamer, alone, from Boston to Provincetown and also returns by ship. Travels to Fire Island on an unsuccessful mission to retrieve body and manuscripts of the shipwrecked Margaret Fuller.

1851 Lectures frequently, at places like Clinton, Medford, Worcester, on topics like Cape Cod, Walden, and "The Wild." Helps runaway slave Henry Williams through the Underground Railroad.

1852 Returns to Walden Pond frequently for material for "The Ponds" section of the Walden manuscript.

1853 First three of proposed five chapters of "A Yankee in Canada" published in *Putnam's Monthly Magazine*, but disagreement with editor and old friend George William Curtis over censorship causes withdrawal of last two. Second trip to Maine Woods. Remaining 706 copies of *A Week* delivered to Thoreau by publisher, who claims he no longer has storage space.

1854   In retaliation for passage of the Kansas-Nebraska Act, Bostonians try to protect fugitive slave Anthony Burns from seizure. Thoreau responds with angry "Slavery in Massachusetts" speech, published first in William Lloyd Garrison's *Liberator* and then in Horace Greeley's *New York Tribune*, most widely read newspaper in the country. *Walden* published by Ticknor and Fields, 9 August, in an edition of 2,000.

1855   Articles on Cape Cod appear serially, June, July, August in *Putnam's Monthly Magazine*. Receives $51.60 as royalty on *Walden*.

1856   On surveying job in Perth Amboy, New Jersey, takes side trip to New York with Bronson Alcott to meet Walt Whitman. First photograph taken, by Benjamin Maxham, the daguerreotype on which most portraits (including the frontispiece in this volume) are based.

1857   Makes last trip, alone this time, to Cape Cod in June. In July travels to Maine woods with Edward Hoar; canoes on Allegash and East Branch with Indian guide Joe Polis. Meets John Brown.

1858   Section of Maine woods experience published in *Atlantic Monthly*, but James Russell Lowell, the editor who had solicited the piece, censors a sentence about a pine tree going to heaven. Thoreau writes him an angry, unanswered letter.

1859   Father dies at 71, leaving Thoreau head of family and of graphite business. Occupied for many weeks after with John Brown's 16 October raid on Harper's Ferry. On 30 October gives speech published the next year as "A Plea for Captain John Brown."

1860   "The Last Days of John Brown," written for the memorial service, published 27 July in *Liberator*. Delivers lecture before Concord Lyceum on 8 February, later published as "Wild Apples." On 20 September reads paper on "The Succession of Forest Trees" to Middlesex Agricultural Society, published the following month in New York *Weekly Tribune*, probably his greatest contribution to natural history. While counting rings on tree stumps in December, contracts a cold that develops into severe bronchitis.

1861   Health declines sharply as bronchitis becomes tuberculosis. Last journal entry 3 November.

1862   Negotiates with James T. Fields, new editor of *Atlantic Monthly*, to publish some lectures as articles. *Atlantic* accepts and pays for "Autumnal Tints," "Life without Principle," "Walking," and "Wild Apples." Asks Ticknor and Fields to take over remaining copies of *A Week* and to drop the subtitle "Or, Life in the Woods" from pending reissue of *Walden*. Dies 6 May, at peace with himself and the world; "Moose" and "Indian" are last words. For funeral ceremonies, 9 May, Bronson Alcott instructs Concord teachers to dismiss pupils, and Emerson reads eulogy.

1863   *Excursions*, first of four posthumous volumes edited by Sophia Thoreau and Ellery Channing published. Contains Emerson's eulogy as preface; early essays, mainly from *Dial*; and late ones, mainly from *Atlantic Monthly*.

1864   *The Maine Woods*.

1865   *Cape Cod*. Emerson's edition of *Letters to Various Persons* published, providing the occasion for James Russell Lowell's influential, largely negative assessment of Thoreau's works.

1866   *A Yankee in Canada with the Anti-Slavery and Reform Papers*, edited by Sophia Thoreau and Ellery Channing.

1881   *Early Spring in Massachusetts*, first compilation of journal entries edited by Thoreau's disciple H. G. O. Blake, who became literary executor after Sophia Thoreau's death. This volume would be followed by three others: *Summer* (1884), *Winter* (1887), *Autumn* (1892).

1893   Ten-volume Riverside Edition of works published by Houghton Mifflin.

1906   Houghton Mifflin issues the 20 volume Walden Edition. Last 14 volumes are the "complete" *Journal*—or least as much as is available at the time and not included in previous books—edited by Francis Allen and Bradford Torrey.

Literary and Historical Context

1

The Two Americas and Transcendentalism

At first glance it would seem that *Walden* is a book that makes its historical context as irrelevant as possible. It appears to be a calculated withdrawal from its surroundings, an obstinate vow "not to live in this restless, nervous, bustling, trivial Nineteenth Century" (329). Some of its most poetic passages evoke a kind of stellar isolation, a one-person act of secession from all American, or even earthly, vicissitudes: "Both place and time were changed, and I dwelt nearer to those parts of the universe and to those eras in history which had most attracted me. Where I lived was as far off as many a region viewed nightly by astronomers. We are wont to imagine rare and delectable places in some remote and more celestial corner of the system, behind the constellation of Cassiopeia's Chair, far from noise and disturbance. I discovered that my house actually had its site in such a withdrawn, but forever new and unprofaned, part of the universe" (87–88). This passage follows a pattern we encounter often in the book: something is first fantasized or envisioned ("We are wont to imagine . . ."), and then through rearranging our ordinary habits of perception and through hard work, it is brought into being, made part of or seen as part of our immediate reality. To use terms from *Walden* itself, we reduce a fact of the imagination to a fact of our understanding (11).

The paradox here, though, is that the terms of this escape from history—indeed, the very notion of escape itself—are profoundly shaped by the historical contexts supposedly left behind. If *Walden* is a retreat from a civilization perceived as stifling, exhausted, and rigidly conventional to some fresher, more vitalizing experience in nature, so too in our mythological consciousness is America itself. For the earliest settlers, the moribund culture was European, and it was later from Britain that we had to declare our independence. But as these American communities themselves became "settled," that is, became routinely predictable and domesticated, both individuals and groups within them yearned to escape, both imaginatively and actually, most often in a westward direction. And these fugitives, of course, created their own settlements, from which they or others then soon had to escape. Yet these escapes were each seen, at least by the escapees, not as withdrawals from America itself but as new attempts in the name of some truer ideal of America that had been lost in the actual acts of settlement.

To see Thoreau's retreat to Walden Pond, then, as a repudiation of American values is to underestimate how complex and contradictory those values are. As Thoreau himself is aware, he is no more thoroughly American than when he denounces the materialism and complacency of his compatriots and withdraws from them to establish his own settlement. He begins this experiment on "Independence Day, or the fourth of July," perhaps "by accident" (84) as he claims, but it is certainly no coincidence that he mentions this date three times in such a deliberately constructed book (45, 59, 84). Further, *Walden* is thick with references to the early settlers of America, particularly to their problems in securing food and shelter, and to Native Americans as a source of solutions to these problems. Far from withdrawing from the American experiment, Thoreau intends to replicate it in microcosm, but this time to get it right. In terms of physical scale, the hut by the pond is not a city on a hill; as a symbol of establishing a civilization on certain ideal principles, however, it often takes on epic proportions, as when a young Irishman watching Thoreau cart off boards comes "to represent spectatordom, and help make this seemingly insignificant event one with the removal of the gods of Troy" (44), a reference to the founding of the Roman Empire. Virtually everything about building this house is seemingly insignificant until one sees it in the light of American aspirations and ideals. Those boards, for example, are taken down to the shore of Walden to be spread on the grass, "there to bleach and warp back again in the sun" (44), as if to remind us that any "new" experiment necessarily begins with old cultural materials—myths, literary traditions, a language—that have to be taken apart, reseen, unwarped, and then combined anew.

Walden, then, is most thoroughly American in its heartbreaking awareness of the gap between American ideals and the immediate social and political realities betraying that ideal at every turn. At one point Thoreau reflects upon another Irish immigrant who "rated it as a gain in coming to America, that here you could get tea, and coffee, and meat every day. But the only true America is that country where you are at liberty to pursue such a mode of life as may enable you to do without these, and where the state does not endeavor to compel you to sustain the slavery and war and other superfluous expenses which directly or indirectly result from the use of such things" (205). To Thoreau, "the only true America" is not the land of material comforts it has been mistaken for but a realm of freedom radically at odds with institutions like slavery and wars that expand its domain. Although it may seem perverse or disproportionate to link these issues in parallel syntactic form with the freedom to abstain from caffeine and flesh, Thoreau sees a correlation between rescuing from unthinking habit even the smallest details of our lives and reconceiving American ideals on the largest scale. He also sees the very desire for physical luxuries in abundance that America blandishes to be in direct contradiction to more spiritual American promises of freedom, equality, and peace. The attempt to create, to give a local habitation to "the only true America," both by the shores of Walden Pond and in the book named for it, is part of a long American tradition of antitraditionalism. For all its solitary individualism, *Walden* is a how-to book for embodying a community that lies in our hopes and fantasies, the land Allen

Ginsberg once called "the lost America of love." This community is one conjured up by a series of visionary texts that precede and follow *Walden*, texts like Thomas Morton's *New English Canaan*, the Declaration of Independence, the Bill of Rights, Walt Whitman's *Leaves of Grass*, Hart Crane's *The Bridge*, Zora Neale Hurston's *Their Eyes Were Watching God*, Gary Snyder's *Earth House Hold*, and Thomas Pynchon's *Vineland*. Like Simon and Garfunkel's cars on the New Jersey turnpike, they've all come to look for America, an America that never really existed but that has persisted on the horizons of our imagination despite centuries of brutal betrayal.

During the writing of *Walden*, between 1845 when Thoreau moved to the pond and 1854 when the book was published, the gap between these two Americas was particularly and agonizingly manifest. Not only did the U.S. government provoke a war with Mexico to extend its empire and increase slave territory, but 1854 also saw passage of the Kansas-Nebraska Act, which rolled back earlier restrictions on slavery and initiated the border violence that would flame into civil war. Less apocalyptic but no less important reminders of the gap were everywhere. The first Women's Rights Convention, held in Seneca Falls in 1848, reminded Americans of the oppressive literalness of the Declaration's "All men are created equal." That same year gold was discovered in California, precipitating the rush that evinced the greed and materialism underlying America's moralistic pieties. A less dramatic but ultimately more significant rush was the one to build railroads. The Fitchburg Railroad, which almost forms a tangent to Walden Pond, was barely finished before Thoreau moved there.

Walden, then, is not as detached and isolated as the "Both place and time were changed . . ." (87) quotation might suggest. It is an attempt to build, as Richard Poirier, borrowing from Shakespeare, has aptly said of all our American classics, "a world elsewhere,"[1] but that world exists in dialectical relationship to the one right here, as the book itself suggests. Thoreau reminds us, for example, that others have lived at Walden, and not completely with the same deliberate freedom in their choice as his. Many are those society has pushed to the margins: slaves and ex-slaves, paupers, drunkards. At the pond the railroad is heard and seen frequently, day and night, and Thoreau meditates on how it is changing not only the face of the country but also our sense of time and space. He can scarcely go out to hoe his beans without hearing the rifle shots of men training for the Mexican War; nor can he go to the village to retrieve a mended shoe without being clapped in jail for refusing to support "the state which buys and sells men, women, and children, like cattle at the door of its senate-house" (171). Even those seemingly detached moments of pure being like the one described in the first passage imply judgments about the society—that it is, for example, old and profaned—for the house at the pond is really a bridge teetering across a chasm between the only true America and the one Thoreau lives in.

$$\bullet \quad \bullet \quad \bullet$$

Thoreau, of course, was not alone in his attempt at bridge building. Jacksonian America was an age of reform and reformers, as *Walden* itself bears witness to in its generally negative comments on them. But Thoreau himself was inevitably seen as a "transcendentalist," as part of the group that most articulately, if not most effectively, tried to close this gap between the potential spirit of America and the institutions constantly belying and stunting that spirit. Put simply, the transcendentalists were a small group of men and a few women who flourished, or tried to, around the Boston and Concord area, most perceptibly from the mid-1830s to the mid-1840s. They were bound to one another more through friendships and associations than through subscribing to the same beliefs: "Thus, by mere attraction of affinity, grew together the brotherhood of the 'Like-minded,' as they were pleasantly nicknamed by outsiders, and by themselves, on the ground that no two were of the same opinion."[2] Despite occasional foolishness and foppery, they deserve to be called radical intellectuals, because like their contemporary, Karl Marx, they felt that the task of philosophy was not to explain the world but to change it. Bronson Alcott, for example, considered the most abstruse and ethereal of them, was active as an educational reformer and had to close one of his experimental schools because he included a black student. Margaret Fuller, who supposedly once walked into a tree because she "saw it but didn't realize it," wrote the first important feminist document in America and showed great physical courage and energy as reporter of and participant in the Italian Revolution. Another group, led by George Ripley, thrived for a while at the alternative community of Brook Farm.

But if the transcendentalists' actions, however utopian or subversive, were clear, to most contemporary Americans their beliefs were far less so. The very bewilderment became an occasion for satire, as when one Baltimore clergyman said that "a new philosophy has risen, maintaining that nothing is everything in general, and everything is nothing in particular." Also in circulation was the story of a teacher— traveling on a Mississippi steamboat—who explained it as follows: "See the holes made in the bank yonder by the swallows. Take away the bank, and leave the apertures, and this is Transcendentalism." And even a more friendly Nathaniel Hawthorne, who had lived at Brook Farm, spent his honeymoon years in Concord, and gone walking and boating with Thoreau, could write in his updated version of *Pilgrim's Progress*: "He is a German by birth, is called Giant Transcendentalist; but as to his form, his features, his substance, and his nature generally, it is the chief peculiarity of this huge miscreant, that neither he for himself, nor anybody for him, has ever been able to describe them. As we rushed by the cavern's mouth, we caught a hasty glimpse of him, looking somewhat like a heap of fog and duskiness. He shouted after us, but in so strong a phraseology that we knew not what he meant, nor whether to be encouraged or affrighted."[3]

The German birth, the smokescreen phraseology, and the indefiniteness of shape and disposition stem from the transcendentalists' interest in Kant and the idealist philosophers that followed him, especially as these philosophers were interpreted and championed by the British writers Samuel Taylor Coleridge and, later, Thomas Carlyle. Although the "transcendentalists" accepted this tag only reluctantly— for they were more concerned with the immanence of spirit in this world than its condition in some other—Emerson made a virtue of necessity by explaining the term as follows:

The Two Americas and Transcendentalism

> It is well known to most of my audience, that the Idealism of the present day acquired the name of Transcendentalism, from the use of that term by Immanuel Kant, of Königsberg, who replied to the skeptical philosophy of Locke, which insisted that there was nothing in the intellect which was not previously in the experience of the senses, by showing that there was a very important class of ideas, or imperative forms, which did not come by experience, but through which experience was acquired; that these were intuitions of the mind itself; and he denominated them *Transcendental* forms. The extraordinary profoundness and precision of that man's thinking have given vogue to his nomenclature, in Europe and America, to that extent, that whatever belongs to the class of intuitive thought, is popularly called at the present day *Transcendental*.[4]

Emerson describes here what some today would call a paradigm shift—a major reconception of the relations between mind and matter. The epistemology of John Locke, accepted so widely in England and America that it became a set of unquestioned assumptions, held that mind is shaped by matter, that it begins as a blank slate, the famous tabula rasa, and is written on by the various impressions that entered through the senses. Kant, on the other hand, felt that the world appears in the form it does to us through and by the structure of the mind itself, that certain categories, such as space, time, and causality exist before—that is, a priori—what we are conscious of as experience.

The emotional center of the transcendentalist challenge, though, lay not in the serenity and complexity of philosophical discourse. Several transcendentalists, notably Ralph Waldo Emerson, Theodore Parker, and George Ripley, had been trained as ministers in the Unitarian church. The Unitarians considered themselves, with justification, the most modern and open of sects and indeed were known as the Liberal Christians. They jettisoned Puritan notions of Original Sin and Predestination but retained the focus on the individual conscience. The Unitarians saw human reason as the best foundation for faith but also believed in the historical reality of biblical events, especially the miracles performed by Jesus. These miracles were God's way of evincing to humanity—through the Lockean senses—the existence of a spiritual realm.

The transcendentalists became increasingly frustrated with the rationalism and social complacency of their elders and found in this inconsistency—that the universe runs on scientifically discernible natural laws except for biblical moments of suspension—a particular vulnerability. By extending—or misunderstanding, as some would say— Kant's notions, they argued that each person could know religious truths intuitively and directly, bypassing not only the Bible, the church, and its institutions but even the senses themselves. Whether biblical miracles occurred and, if so, which ones were authentic—a major project of Unitarian scholarship—was irrelevant to these intuitions of a more immediate and continual spiritual reality. Emerson could call Locke's philosophy "skeptical," even though Locke was a sincere and orthodox Christian, because it left no room for these direct apprehensions of the divine.

Carried to its logical, or, rather, supralogical conclusion, transcendentalism could dispense with Christ himself as the bearer of divine truth, or at best see him as an exemplar or metaphor of the fact that the divine forever incarnates itself in the human, in all humans. And it was in taking this step in the graduation address Emerson delivered to Harvard Divinity School's class of 1838 that he put the Liberal Christians in the uncomfortable position of declaring some of its brightest younger members infidels: "[Jesus] spoke of miracles; for he felt that man's life was a miracle, and all that man doth, and he knew that this daily miracle shines, as the character ascends. But the word Miracle, as pronounced by Christian churches, gives a false impression; it is Monster. It is not one with the blowing clover and the falling rain" (Emerson, 80).

Thoreau was a half-generation younger than most of these men who left or were driven from Unitarianism. He met many of them through his friendship with Emerson, who had begun to live at Concord while Thoreau was in Cambridge, studying at Harvard College. Although Thoreau found the meetings of the Transcendental Club too genteel and rarefied for his tastes, he did form close personal and intellectual friendships with some of its members, notably Alcott, who later moved to Concord himself. The exact relation of *Walden* to transcendentalism has been debated. At one extreme, the book is seen as the artistic culmination of the movement, its one indisputable book-length masterpiece. At the other, it is seen as a significant break, even a refutation, especially of transcendentalism's metaphysical predilection for spirit over matter and its minimizing of the senses. But wherever one eventually comes out on this issue, it is important to see the transcendentalist context as the enabling condition for Thoreau's work. It was enabling in the sense of providing both an immediate context for Thoreau's career as a writer and a structure of ideas and attitudes through which he could begin to approach the world.

Much of the former was provided by Ralph Waldo Emerson, the movement's leading writer and lecturer. While Thoreau was a senior at Harvard in 1837, he had read Emerson's first book, *Nature*, and began a personal friendship that year on returning to Concord. Emerson gave Thoreau the crucial advice to begin a writer's journal and, later, when the *Dial*, the transcendentalist organ, began in 1840, pressed Thoreau's submissions on its sometimes reluctant editor, Margaret Fuller. When Emerson himself took over the editorship two years later, he nurtured what he correctly perceived to be Thoreau's potential as a nature writer by assigning him to review a series of reports commissioned by the state of Massachusetts on its birds, beasts, and plants. Emerson also employed Thoreau as a live-in handyman when he and his brother John had to close their school because of the latter's ill health—a move that gave Thoreau even more access to Emerson's library and conversation. And it was on land Emerson had just bought by the shores of Walden that Thoreau began his most famous experiment in living and writing. That the two men had a falling-out in the ensuing years, each feeling unappreciated and misunderstood by the other, should not diminish the energizing and sustaining nature of the friendship on both sides in its early years.

Just as he built his hut on Emerson's land, Thoreau built much of his writing on the substructure of transcendentalism. He did not, for example, have to expend energy in the theological joustings with Unitarianism that Emerson initiated and Ripley and Parker pursued but could instead begin directly to explore religious experiences outside

the bounds of Christianity, to read without defensiveness or conde-
scension the Oriental scriptures, and to seek divinity immediately in
nature. Emerson's "American Scholar," his address to Thoreau's college class of 1837, is a compendium of other ways in which transcendentalism was liberating for the young writer. Although the speech has
become best known for its plea for a native literature and intellectual
tradition, by this time the plea had itself become something of a formu-
laic genre in American oratory. More radical is its delineation of the
three main influences on the scholar: nature, books, and action. Of
the first Emerson relates the human mind to the natural world, so that
"the ancient precept, 'Know thyself,' and the modern precept, 'Study
nature,' become at last one maxim" (Emerson, 56). Instead of the
expected encomium about book learning, Emerson stresses the paradox of how creative thought becomes rigidified and then overly rever-
enced in the process of becoming a book. "Genius," then, "is always
sufficiently the enemy of genius by over influence" (Emerson, 58). A
more productive force for genuine knowledge and expression is direct
action, preferably physical labor in the world of nature: "What is lost
in seemliness is gained in strength. Not out of those, on whom systems
of education have exhausted their culture, comes the helpful giant to
destroy the old or to build the new, but out of unhandselled savage
nature, out of terrible Druids and Berserkirs, come at last Alfred and
Shakespeare" (Emerson, 62).

Transcendentalism, then, especially in its Emersonian formulations, creates a set of ironies. One cannot be its follower or disciple
anymore than one can organize an association of anarchists. Its own
writings have to be seen as ultimately disposable, of little value compared with that of the active, creating soul. Its advocacy of a kind of
uncompromising self-trust would seem to undermine any basis for
community. And yet both as a loose intellectual community and as a
loose convergence of ideas, transcendentalism provided a space where
a young writer could practice without becoming a disciple, an echo
chamber to first discern and then extend one's own voice. Thus, it is
important not to mistake the voices of *Walden* as emanating from an
isolated void but to hear in them also the voices of American culture

and its transcendentalist subculture, inflected and modulated by an individual for whom radical individualism was not just a creed but an entire way of being in the world.

If *Walden*, then, is a jeremiad calling for a retreat from the corruptions of American society, it is so in a characteristically American way. Thoreau, the village eccentric of a culture that both values and punishes extreme individuality, isolated himself from his compatriots only to write a book the accents of which have become strangely familiar to us.

2

The Importance of the Work

In other volumes of this series, the chapter corresponding to this one tells you how crucial its subject is to Western civilization in general and to your education in particular. While such remarks are surely valid in each case, they are sometimes counterproductive when aimed at the first-time reader, creating either unnecessary awe or an expectation of boredom and stodginess. Such advertising is further superfluous because you either have been assigned the book for a course or are reading it for your own enjoyment, both motives that should not be tampered with. I was tempted to title this volume "*Walden*": *Not a Great Book*, for although I have always felt it is a great book, I have also felt it is too playful, too provocative, too subversive to be approached as a monument. *Walden* needs to be rescued from the required-reading lists of the cultural conservatives, for it does not so much teach eternal verities—if indeed there are such things—as it exercises the inquisitive, skeptical mind that takes nothing on authority, including itself and books of literary criticism. To approach *Walden* as merely the acquisition of a piece of cultural literacy is to take it in a spirit completely opposed to the ideals of the "American Scholar" sketched in chapter 1.

The Importance of the Work

What I would offer as the main reason for reading *Walden*, then, is the quality and intensity of that reading experience itself. I aspire to be like the Zen teacher who when asked "What is the essence of water?" threw the student into the pond. This is not to say that the experience of reading is undiscussable—indeed, the opposite is the premise of this book—but, rather, that *Walden* does not lend itself to easy preliminary generalizations. *Walden* should be first probed and analyzed in detail, across individual words, sentences, paragraphs, and chapters. I have quoted liberally from the book itself in the belief that the best way to understand its most resonant passages is to reread them often and deliberately.

That said, there are two important areas not emphasized in the rest of this book that I will highlight here. The first is that the experience of reading *Walden* should be more than just literary and intellectual. The book is quite serious about asking you to change your life. And if you do not change it, you are at least challenged to be able to think it through, to give an account of it in the same specificity and scope as Thoreau does his. I find, however, that Thoreau's long opening discussion of the economics of living is about as clear, witty, and penetrating as anyone could wish. It is also often cranky, petulant, and repetitive. For me to try to summarize or paraphrase these sections in language that almost necessarily would be more academic or more anemic would be to make them sound even more preachy and long-winded than they are. And so I will only say here, take Thoreau seriously as well as humorously: "Economy is a subject which admits of being treated with levity, but it cannot so be disposed of" (29).

The second point is that no matter how much the Zen teacher might wish it, no American can come to the reading of *Walden* pure, free of preconceptions; the image of Thoreau living in a hut by the pond has become a cultural icon, with instant name recognition, as in Walden Puddle or Waldenbooks. As we have seen in chapter 1, the book embodies the quintessential American situation of a self-reliant individual starting a new life in a new land. In recent years Thoreau has also become a prophet of ecology, and a counter for both radical political activism and complete withdrawal from society. For better or worse, his own person has become both an archetype and a stereotype. One effect of this situation is that Thoreau gets blamed for violating goals or creeds he never established for himself. For example, he is skewered for using matches to start fires or eating meals at the homes of friends or using Emerson's land, while he himself does not set out rigid doctrines of primitivism or complete self-sufficiency; he even tells us that he has borrowed an ax and that "it is the most generous course thus to permit your fellow-men to have an interest in your enterprise" (41). It is not that Thoreau is free of his own crotchets, especially those about chastity—and here we can say only that chastity is its own punishment—but that we should know which are really his and which have been projected on him. One of the better reasons for spending time with *Walden* is to discover the complexities, even contradictions, of Thoreau's own vision instead of mistaking it for the cultural slogans and cartoons. Read the book, not the bumper sticker!

The powerful cultural valence of *Walden* can be seen in the current battle over developing two woodland areas around the pond. The town of Concord, where Thoreau is often still remembered as an oddball woodsburner, had approved plans to construct an office build- ing on Brister's Hill and condominiums on Bear Garden Hill. But these plans have been challenged, and perhaps even thwarted, by a national alliance of Thoreauvians and environmentalists, the Walden Woods Project, which hopes to raise enough money to buy and conserve the land in question. One of its most interesting efforts has been the publication of *Heaven Is Under Our Feet*, a collection of essays by celebrities, politicians, and authors—including Don Henley, Jimmy Carter, Paula Abdul, Whoopi Goldberg, and Louise Erdrich.[1] While many of these writers treat "Thoreau" simply as one who stands for ecological values, it is surprising and heartening how many have read in him widely and lovingly over a period of years.

But while there is no doubt about who is on the side of the angels here, we have to ask whether the conservationists have also missed part of the spirit of *Walden*—the book, not the pond—for it is really not these particular woodlands or this particular author that needs to be sanctified and enshrined. I remember my initial disappointment of first seeing Walden Pond. The pond was pleasant but did not have the peculiar shimmering aura I had imagined from reading the book—hundreds of similar spots in New England and elsewhere are as quietly beautiful. And that, I came to realize, was the point: that any place perceived and written about with such appetite and intensity is as sacred, that "Olympus is but the outside of the earth every where" (85). The importance of *Walden*, then, is not as a cultural or natural shrine, but rather an experience in the lives of its readers.

3

Composition and Reception

W_alden_ is one of those works that epitomize an author's life and writing, that gather all rays on a single focal point. Such books— among them *The Scarlet Letter, Moby-Dick*, and *Huckleberry Finn*— make everything else the author did seem like a preparation or a falling off. Robert Frost, with some envy, describes the situation: "A man may write well and very well all his life, yet only once in a lifetime have such luck with him in the choice of a subject—a real gatherer, to which everything in him comes tumbling. Thoreau's immortality may hang by a single book, but the book includes even his writing that is *not* in it. Nothing he ever said but sounds like a quotation from it. Think of the success of a man's pulling himself together all under one one-word title."[1] Frost was acute in citing luck as a key factor, for as we look more closely at the composition and publication of Thoreau's work, we can see that Thoreau initially did not think of *Walden* as his magnum opus. It was neither the book he first went to the pond to write nor the one he planned to spend as much time on as he eventually did over a period of nine years. From our point of view—namely, hindsight—things seem to have broken just right for the composition of *Walden*, but certainly not in a way its author would have seen as fortunate at the time. Thoreau probably would have preferred that the book become just one in a long career instead of becoming that career itself in the eyes of many readers. Although examining the composition of *Walden* will not lay bare all of the mysteries of artistic creation, it can make us more informed and responsive readers of the book as it now stands. The subject is particularly relevant, since—as chapters 4 and 5 of this book will elaborate—one of the central themes of *Walden* is its own writing, especially the relations of this writing to the experiences lived around and through it.

"My purpose in going to Walden Pond was not to live cheaply nor to live dearly there, but to transact some private business" (19). Insofar as this private business can be specified, it was the writing of Thoreau's first book, *A Week on the Concord and Merrimack Rivers.* The sense in which it is private was its hidden purpose as a memorial tribute to his brother John, also his closest friend, who had died agonizingly of tuberculosis and lockjaw in 1842. It was John who had been Henry's companion in the 1839 vacation trip that provides the frame for this book, actually a two-week boating and hiking expedition through Massachusetts and New Hampshire. Though John's name is never mentioned, he remains a shadowy presence in the book, and several of the long digressions, like the one on friendship, touch on him indirectly.

As the idea of *A Week* coalesced in Thoreau's mind, he found difficulties in executing it. He was living in large, bustling households—first his parents' boardinghouse and then as a handyman at the Emersons'—and had trouble finding the quiet, uninterrupted stretches of time he needed. A solution suggested itself when in 1844 Emerson bought some land, variously known as the Briars and Wyman's Field, by the shores of Walden Pond. Thoreau had long thought of building a small house for himself on the shores of a pond, an idea already realized by his Harvard classmate, Charles Stearns Wheeler, who did so near Sandy, or Flint's, Pond, where Thoreau visited for two weeks in the summer of 1837.

The move to Walden turned out to be psychologically sustaining and creatively productive. Thoreau left the pond two years, two months, and two days later with the completed manuscript of *A Week* and a first draft of *Walden*, as well as essays on Thomas Carlyle and on his own ascent of Mount Kaatdn in the Maine woods, both of which were first delivered as lectures and then published in magazines. Thoreau's expectations of literary fame, though, began to be severely qualified as both Emerson and he tried unsuccessfully to interest a publisher in *A Week*. Evert Duyckinck, a mentor of Melville and at that time an editor at Wiley and Putman, enthusiastically recommended the book; however, the firm offered to publish it only at the author's expense. Thoreau received similar terms from other publishers, including Ticknor and Company, which did, though, express a lively interest in publishing *Walden*. Finally, Thoreau accepted the terms offered by James Munroe because this firm allowed him to pay expenses out of author's royalties instead of advancing the sum.

A Week on the Concord and Merrimack Rivers, then, was published on 30 May 1849, 2 years after it had been largely completed and 10 years after the events it narrates. Although it was reviewed fairly widely and generally favorably in both the United States and England—*Godey's Lady's Book* mistook it for a work by John Greenleaf Whittier—it did not sell. Not only were Thoreau's hopes for literary fame deflated, but he found himself in debt for $290. Four years later Thoreau recorded in his journal the following short history of its publication:

> For a year or two past, my *publisher*, falsely so called, has been writing from time to time to ask what disposition should be made of the copies of "A Week on the Concord and Merrimack Rivers" still on hand, and at last suggesting that he had use for the room they occupied in his cellar. So I had them all sent to me here, and they have arrived to-day by express, filling the man's wagon,—706 copies out of an edition of 1000 which I bought of Munroe four years ago and have been ever since paying for, and have not quite paid for yet. The wares are sent to me at last, and I have an opportunity to examine my purchase. They are something more substantial than fame, as my back knows, which has borne them up two flights of stairs to a place similar to that to which they trace their origin. Of the remaining two hundred and ninety odd, seventy-five were given away, the rest sold. I have now a library of nearly nine hundred volumes, over seven hundred of which I wrote myself.
>
> —*Journal*, V:459

Composition and Reception

A Week carried in its back pages an advertisement for *Walden*, which it claimed would appear soon. But because the financial fortunes of the former book were hardly enough to interest Munroe or any other publisher in issuing the latter, and because Thoreau himself was even less able to finance the venture, *Walden* was not published until 1854, almost a decade after it was begun. During that time it went through seven drafts: three to polish the original conception and, after a virtual hiatus of three years, four more drafts after 1852 that substantially widened and altered the initial versions. It could be said, then, that the financial failure of *A Week* helped make *Walden* the artistic success it is. It not only gave Thoreau more time to think and write, but it made him radically reevaluate how to live a writer's life: he could no longer gamble on the sale of his books to support him; rather, he had to live so simply and economically as to grant himself leisure to write the kinds of books that do not sell. And the Walden experience could be seen as offering a blueprint or at least an example of such a life. After telling the story of an Indian who thought that all he had to do was weave baskets and it would be the white man's job to buy them, Thoreau writes in *Walden*: "I too had woven a kind of basket of a delicate texture, but I had not made it worth any one's while to buy them. Yet not the less, in my case, did I think it worth my while to weave them, and instead of studying how to make it worth men's while to buy my baskets, I studied rather how to avoid the necessity of selling them" (19).

The story of *Walden*'s composition might have been lost to us were it not for the literary detective work of J. Lyndon Shanley. Scholars who had examined the mound of draft material before he did found no discernible order and concluded that Thoreau was among the sloppiest of writers. But Shanley discovered that he could reorder the leaves, on the basis of watermarks and handwriting, into seven distinct versions. The person responsible for the mess was not the author but a careless early editor, Franklin Sanborn, who had wrenched the manuscripts around to put together his own version of the book padded with unpublished material. Shanley published his ideas on the composition of the book based on his reading of the seven versions he had reconstructed, along with a text of the first version in

The Making of Walden,[2] and later Ronald Clapper produced a genetic text that made available to other scholars all the changes throughout the seven versions.[3]

Shanley showed that the bulk of the later additions appear in what is now the second half of the book, and that they served to fill out, especially with fall and winter passages, the cycle of the seasons that was in Thoreau's mind from the start. Yet because Thoreau did not revise the earlier passages with a view toward any philosophical or psychological consistency, later scholars have read *Walden* not just as the story of one or two years at the pond but as a kind of inner autobiography that, through the incorporation of journal passages, stretches from his thoughts several years before he moved to the pond to facts and ideas discovered right up to proofreading in 1854. In general, as the book and the years go on Thoreau seems to be less interested in social concerns than in the workings and moods of his own mind; he comes to view nature as more ambiguous and impenetrable, more alien, than he had in the earlier years and chapters. *Walden*, then, could be said to be written in the "first people" rather than in the first person; in its final version, it is something of a palimpsest that includes a variety of shifting viewpoints and voices. Robert Sattelmeyer, who has studied its composition most recently and most perceptively, argues that the book is stronger for this: "Much of the richness of the book ultimately derives, I believe, from Thoreau's incorporation of reflections from the intervening years that are allowed to stand alongside accounts that he actually wrote at the pond, so that *Walden* is at once both retrospective and dramatic. It embodies a summing but not a summing up of experience."[4]

Alongside this intellectual and psychological development, we can see as we read the manuscript versions and the journals a writer increasingly conscious and exploitative of the writing process itself. Thoreau was disappointed in the way *A Week* was pieced together by combining separate journal entries first into lectures and then into essays and chapters: "And at last they stand like the cubes of Pythagoras firmly on either basis—like statues on their pedestals—but the statues rarely take hold of hands— There is only such connexion and series as is attainable in the galleries" (*Journal*, 2:205–6). But his work on *Walden* gave him the opposite experience of ideas and sentences meshing into place, creating a whole more dynamic and complex than its parts: "Thoughts accidentally thrown together become a frame in which more may be developed and exhibited. . . . Having by chance recorded a few disconnected thoughts and then brought them into juxtaposition, they suggest a whole new field in which it was possible to labor and to think" (*Journal*, III:217).

Thoreau seems to have trained himself to take advantage of discoveries that can be made by pushing words and sentences together or pulling them apart. For example, what seems to be a straightforward statement in the journal—"I have travelled some in New England, especially in Concord"—turns into a resonant pun and paradox in revision—"I have travelled a good deal in Concord" (4). On a larger scale, the passage about the clay thawing in "Spring" is made to yield all kinds of further insights through the actual writing and rewriting of it, down to the shapes and significances of letters within words. In several senses, then, the delay in publishing *Walden* gave Thoreau the leisure to write as he pleased.

• • •

As a financial enterprise, *Walden* did little better than *A Week*. While 1,744 copies out of a pressrun of 2,000 were sold the first year, it would take 5 more years to sell the rest. In its first 15 years, sales averaged only 300 hundred per year. That record is somewhat surprising, since the initial reviews of this book too were strongly positive, if not perceptively appreciative. Conventional scholarly wisdom has perpetuated the notion that *Walden* was poorly received in the contemporary press, a notion refuted by the most recent compilation of reviews which publishes 56 pieces previously unknown to modern scholarship. As the compilers write, "By the end of August 1854, *Walden* had in fact been praised in over thirty magazines from Maine to Ohio . . . Of the sixty-six contemporary reviews that have been located, forty-six were strongly favorable."[5]

But while the reviewers enjoyed and recommended *Walden*, they seemed often to not quite know what to make of its mixtures of voices and forms. The *Worcester Palladium* said, "*Walden* is a prose poem. It has classic elegance, and New England homeliness, with a sprinkle of Oriental magnificence" (16 August 1854). The more widely read *Graham's Magazine* wrote, "Sometimes strikingly original, sometimes merely eccentric and odd, it is always racy and stimulating" (September 1854). Indeed, the stance reviewers most commonly took was to commend the book as a good read but at the same time to pull back from the author's philosophy and way of life, almost always described as quirky or quixotic. One or both of the terms "quaint" and "eccentric" appear in 34 of the 66 reviews. Gamaliel Bailey summed up much of the general attitude in the *National Era* for 28 September 1854, "But with all its extravagances, its sophisms, and its intellectual pride, the book is acute and suggestive, and contains passages of great beauty."

With the relatively wide and generally favorable press and the strenuous publicizing by James T. Fields, the junior partner of Ticknor and Fields, we can only surmise, then, why the book did not sell. One likely reason is that as the reviews suggest, *Walden* did not fit into any clear niche in the literary marketplace. The two most popular genres were novels and travel writing, and Thoreau insults the readers of both in *Walden*. He calls the former "gingerbread" (105), empty calories for the mind, and declares early that he is writing a kind of antitravel book "not so much concerning the Chinese and Sandwich Islanders as you who read these pages, who are said to live in New England" (4). "Said to," because he knows for sure only that they reside there. But the reading public was not so much taking revenge for some insult as they were probably just puzzled as to what kind of book it was. Another common adjective in the reviews was "original," and because the book's philosophy was often described as transcendental or Emersonian, this originality must have had more to do with the form or genre of the book. *Walden* is more the kind of book that creates successors than follows precedents, and so it is less strange to us today after so many nonfiction books of personal experience by writers like Norman Mailer, Edward Abbey, and Annie Dillard. Some see this genealogy as going back to the transcendentalists, as does Henry Miller in his epigraph to *Tropic of Cancer* (1934): "These novels will give way, by and by, to diaries or autobiographies—captivating books, if only a man knew how to choose among what he calls his experiences that which is really his experience, and how to record truth truly.— Ralph Waldo Emerson."[6]

It seems to have taken us some time to learn how to read these books as well. After Thoreau's death in 1862, there was a minor boomlet, both aided by and manifested in the appearance of a few late essays in the *Atlantic Monthly* and five posthumous books in as many years: *Excursions, The Maine Woods, Cape Cod, Letters to Various Persons*, and *A Yankee in Canada*. Moreover, Ticknor and Fields brought out a second edition of *Walden*, honoring Thoreau's request that the subtitle "Or, Life in the Woods" be dropped. Nevertheless, for the rest of the century, there was little demand, for in the midst of this boomlet appeared James Russell Lowell's essay characterizing Thoreau as a crank, a hypocrite, a mere follower of Emerson, and, occasionally, a writer of perfect prose. Lowell's charges were later seconded in England by Robert Louis Stevenson, who added "skulker" to the list and remarked on Thoreau's personal coldness, "It was not inappropriate, surely, that he had such close relations with the fish."[7] With such highly influential literary figures ranged against it, Thoreau's reputation could easily have died out in the nineteenth century.

A year after Stevenson's review, however, in 1881, H. G. O. Blake, who had become literary executor after the death of Thoreau's sister, Sophia, began, with *Early Spring in Massachusetts*, publishing excerpts from Thoreau's 2-million-words-long journal. While these books achieved some popularity, the bad news is that they perpetuated the stereotype of Thoreau as primarily a nature writer, since little else was taken from the journals. Soon after, though, in England, Stevenson wrote a retraction and *Walden* particularly was taken seriously as a piece of social criticism in books by H. A. Page, Henry S. Salt, and Edward Carpenter. Also in the 1890s an American professor of homeopathic medicine, Dr. Samuel A. Jones, began gathering and collating biographical data, often from still-living acquaintances.

For most of the nineteenth century and the beginning of the twentieth, Thoreau was something of a cult author, although different groups of enthusiasts claimed him for different reasons. The 1910s and 1920s, however, saw a major reevaluation of American literature and culture by figures like John Macy, Van Wyck Brooks, and Waldo Frank. These writers chafed at the narrowness and gentility of what was then the canon—Whittier, Bryant, Longfellow, and Lowell—and hoped to replace them with rougher, more authentically native figures like Whitman, Thoreau, and Twain. At this time American writers were just beginning to be taught and studied extensively in the academy, and Norman Foerster, a major force in this movement, secured for Thoreau an early place in it.

Yet despite the work of Foerster, Vernon Parrington, Raymond Adams, and a few others, Thoreau's book was not given the depth and detail of response it deserved until the 1941 publication of F. O. Matthiessen's *American Renaissance: Art and Expression in the Age of Emerson and Whitman*.[8] As is discussed further in chapter 6, Matthiessen argued convincingly for the unity and coherence of *Walden*, and analyzed closely the power and vigor of the language. Matthiessen brought a range of concerns to his work, including cultural criticism; given the critical temper of his time, however, the leads that were followed were primarily those of tracing image clusters and other patterns of connection. Some of Matthiessen's larger concerns were restored to the study of *Walden* by the "myth and symbol" school of American studies in the 1950s and 1960s, when critics like R. W. B. Lewis[9] and Leo Marx[10] showed how these image clusters embody key tensions in American culture at large.

As one who in the past few years has read or reread all of the academic criticism on *Walden*, I have to say that much of it is dreary and repetitive, probably more so than that on other major American figures. The most interesting and substantial work has been more scholarly, more in the way of providing materials to read *Walden* than in giving such readings directly. Shanley's book has already been mentioned, and in 1965 Walter Harding published *The Days of Henry Thoreau*, drawing together his decades of biographical sleuthing.[11]

More recently William Howarth,[12] and Sharon Cameron[13] have presented readings of the Journal, and Robert Richardson[14] and Robert Sattelmeyer[15] have documented extensively Thoreau's reading and intellectual growth. The editors of the Princeton Edition of the writings, now under the direction of Elizabeth Hall Witherell, continue to provide new texts and new discoveries about Thoreau.

Two significant book-length readings of *Walden* rise above the mediocrity of most of the articles on the work. Charles Anderson's *The Magic Circle of "Walden,"* published in 1968, raises Matthiessen's sense of the book's craftsmanship to the highest power, by reading the book as a "poem" and schematizing its design as a web: "Walden Pond lies at the center as a symbol of the purity and harmony yearned for by man, though unattainable. Radial lines of wit run out from this, cutting across the attractions of the purely pragmatic or sensual life. And these radial lines are looped with circle after concentric circle of aspiration towards the ideal life of heaven—which is also mirrored in the central pond."[16] The strength of Anderson's book, though, lies not so much in explaining this design as in his sensitive explications of tone, imagery, and verbal technique in separate passages. Its weakness lies in using this aesthetic approach to blunt or negate other kinds of meaning in the book. Reading *Walden* as a poem, he claims, "the reader can avoid being taken in by the pretended subjects (like the argument against railroads) and so discover the true poetic subjects (like the meaning of solitude)" (Anderson, 17). Yet this notion works against his own argument, because it concedes large chunks of the book to "pretended subjects" and seems to say that *Walden* fits together as a poem perfectly except for those parts which do not.

Stanley Cavell in *The Senses of "Walden"* reads the book no less closely than Anderson but takes seriously—perhaps too seriously in missing the book's playfulness and uncertainties—its moral and social urgency: "It would be a fair summary of the book's motive to say that it invites us to take an interest in our lives, and teaches us how."[17] Cavell is not a literary critic but a philosopher. When his book was first published in 1972, neither discipline showed much interest, but now that literary studies have become more philosophical and vice versa, it has become something of a sleeper. Cavell himself has returned to Thoreau and Emerson in his most recent work, pointing out their boldness as thinkers and suggesting that they have been not just ignored but repressed in American philosophy. Nonetheless, although Cavell's work itself is being highly revalued few scholars have followed his insights in locating Thoreau as a philosopher. Thoreau is still missing from most histories of American philosophy, and even Cornel West's recent book, *The American Evasion of Philosophy: A Genealogy of Pragmatism*, which traces the lines of American thought most congenial to Thoreau, does not mention him.[18] It is to this gap that the last chapter 8 of the present volume tries to speak.

Thoreau's promotion to cultural icon has already been noted. While Anderson was trying to buffer *Walden* from any immediate practical message, his students were turning to Thoreau as a spokesman for and symbol of the uncompromising assertion of principle in the face of institutionalized wrongdoing. In 1970, when the U.S. government began bombing Cambodia and shooting students at Kent State, *The Night Thoreau Spent in Jail* was first produced, and went on to become the most frequently staged play of the decade. This phenomenon prompted little response in academic criticism except the negative reactions of certain scholars who now felt it necessary to trash Thoreau.[19]

Compared to the relative lull of the 1980s, the past two years have seen a small renaissance in academic Thoreau studies. Most notable of this recent work are H. Daniel Peck's *Thoreau's Morning Work*,[20] Henry Golemba's *Thoreau's Wild Rhetoric*,[21] and Frederick Garber's *Thoreau's Fable of Inscribing*.[22] Although these three books are significantly different from each other, they all focus on particular paradoxes, anomalies, and contradictions in Thoreau's work. In this sense, literary criticism can be viewed as catching up with the particular knottiness and playfulness in *Walden*, for contemporary theory helps us see how texts turn back on themselves to question their own apparent meanings, how their nodes of self-conflict reveal more than their clarifications. Golemba's book in particular shows how Thoreau delighted as much in unravelling meaning as in creating it, avoiding the traps of oversimplification and fixity.

Composition and Reception

This very fluidity and elusiveness will continue to provoke readers into creating a *Walden* in their own image. As psychologists tell us, the more ambiguous and complex the stimulus, the more it becomes a screen for own concerns and fantasies. But although we cannot escape this process, we can—as *Walden* itself suggests—become more aware of its workings, of the ways our consciousness of words and the world interpenetrate each other.

A Reading

4

On Reading *Walden*
Suggestions and Provocations

Before proceeding to the detailed reading of *Walden* that takes up the rest of this book, I want to raise certain questions, initially about methodology but ultimately of philosophical and political import. And while answers to these questions can be only tentative and partial, it is the raising of them, not the lowering or suppressing of them, that is crucial. An earlier reading of *Walden* begins promisingly by confronting its own existence in asking, "What hope is there in a book about a book?" (Cavell 1974, v). Assuming there is hope, we can go on to ask what a reading of another book can and cannot do, and what dangers and possibilities exist in the project.

I should begin by saying that I find the format of this series—a set of extended readings of important books—particularly congenial and timely. My own training two decades ago was devoted to close readings of individual works. Since then, literary studies have taken larger perspectives and become more skeptical and theoretical about notions of reading, writing, and interpreting; no longer are areas like philosophy, psychology, and history ruled out of court. Yet this widening of scope has sometimes been at the expense of the kind of passionate attention to how words work in specific contexts that should still be at the center of our inquiries. Some recent instances of literary criticism first make a general point and then simply quote a paragraph from the primary text, as if the quoting itself makes that point, or as if the point itself is the only goal. Many small, local truths are sacrificed to big ideas, although the very notion of big ideas has, ironically, been one of the targets of recent theory. And while I am not interested in returning to the narrowing of literary discourse that once accompanied the practice of close reading, I am grateful for the chance to show that close reading can be put in the service of the larger critical issues with which many of us are now concerned, that the engagement with words on the page is still the central and most exciting part of what we do.

A discussion of reading and interpreting, though, is not just pre-liminary or tangential to a discussion of the book itself, because one of the major subjects of *Walden* is its own writing and reading, as we are alerted to in its first words: "When I wrote the following pages . . ." (3). *Walden* contains an entire chapter on "Reading," one that most critics see as containing instructions for approaching its pages, and is constantly aware of itself as a linguistic structure. While this reflexiveness gives the book a place in the history of literary modern-ism, more important is that it evinces radical thinking about reading and about education central to transcendentalism itself.

This thinking is profoundly anti-institutional, and so it is not surprising that even usually benevolent institutions like the schools and colleges where the book is primarily read do not push hard on its implications. Further, *Walden* is tough-minded enough to be con-cerned about its own gestures toward authority and certainty. We can begin with a sentence that challenges the very idea of literary analysis itself: "The volatile truth of our words should continually betray the inadequacy of the residual statement" (325).

As one ponders this statement, its own words seem to enact their truths rather than invite paraphrase. But part of the meaning is that it is really in the act of thinking, rather than in any final product, that truth resides—or rather, that since truth is necessarily volatile, it is true only while it is in motion, not after it has been fixed and formu-lated. Truth is always larger and more in flux than any static attempt to capture it can render. We should not come to reading with the hope of short-circuiting the entire process of thinking by taking away only the final product, some quintessential bottom line from another's work. The most we can hope for—but it is a great deal—is to become more engaged in the process ourselves and to envision it in terms of our own lives.

This stance helps explain what many students feel is a paradox or contradiction in *Walden*. What is one to make, they ask, of a writer who says, "I have yet to hear the first syllable of valuable or even earnest advice from my seniors" (9), and then goes on in the next few pages to quote Confucius, Samuel Laing, Gookin, Darwin, and Chapman and to praise the ancient Chinese, Hindu, Persian, and Greek philosophers? And even more important, why do we keep reading the syllables of our senior, Henry D. Thoreau, we for whom life is also an experiment untried by us? Part of the answer lies in Thoreau's chapter on "Reading," which, significantly, is named for an activity and not for an object (as in "Classics" or "Books"), for the activity itself is the interface between past and present, the point at which the then becomes the now. In reading we activate the words of others in our own consciousness and in our mind's ear. The written word is "carved out of the breath of life itself. The symbol of an ancient man's thought becomes a modern man's speech" (102).

For Thoreau, then, reading is not a Lockean process of passively absorbing what is already created out there but rather a more transcendentalist one of reciprocity, of mind actively shaping, partaking in creations: "To read well, that is, to read true books in a true spirit, is a noble exercise, and one that will task the reader more than any exercise which the customs of the day esteem. It requires a training such as the athletes underwent, the steady intention almost of the whole life to this object. Books must be read as deliberately and reservedly as they were written" (100–101). This genuine activity, Thoreau says later in the chapter, is not "that which lulls us as a luxury and suffers the nobler faculties to sleep the while, but what we have to stand on tiptoe to read and devote our most alert and wakeful hours to" (104).

It should not detract significantly from Thoreau's achievement here to note that he is stating in a positive way the obverse of Emerson's critique of traditional education and reading in "The American Scholar":

> The sacredness which attaches to the act of creation,—the act of thought,—is transferred to the record. The poet chanting, was felt to be a divine man: henceforth the chant is divine also. The writer was a just and wise spirit: henceforward it is settled, the book is perfect; as love of the hero corrupts into worship of his statue. Instantly, the book becomes noxious: the guide is a tyrant. . . . Colleges are built on it. Books are written on it by thinkers, not by Man Thinking; by men of talent, that is, who start wrong, who set out from accepted dogmas, not from their own sight of principles. Meek young men grow up in libraries, believing it their duty to accept the views, which Cicero, which Locke, which Bacon, have given, forgetful that Cicero, Locke, and Bacon were only young men in libraries, when they wrote these books.
>
> —Emerson, 57

The problems these views create for the writer are incorporated into the very structure of *Walden*, as the next chapter argues, but here we should focus on the problems and opportunities they create for us as readers.

As readers, then, we are called on to give alert, deliberate, painstaking attention to the words before us and yet at the same time not to reverence them unduly, not to take them too unquestioningly. They should be occasions, rather, for our own creation. After the sentence about volatile truths comes the following: "Their truth is instantly *translated*; its literal monument alone remains" (325). Thoreau goes back to etymology, as he often does, for one of his senses of "literal"— quite literally the letters on the page, the physical configurations that initiate meaning. But our task is to apprehend, to replicate a more dynamic motion beyond and through the words, those fixed statues and monuments. In "Reading" Thoreau says it is "worth the expense of youthful days," a large price in his uncompromising economy of living, to learn even a few words of an ancient language, "which are raised out of the trivialness of the street, to be perpetual suggestions and provocations" (100). Later in the same chapter he says of his own writing, "I do not wish to flatter my townsmen, nor to be flattered by them, for that will not advance either of us. We need to be *provoked*— goaded like oxen, as we are, into a trot" (108, emphasis added).

It is not so much, then, that Thoreau has specific facts and ideas he wants simply to transmit from his mind to ours, even if such a thing were possible, for even though he insists on a certain specificity in describing his own life, he knows, first, that such specificity has a limited applicability and, second, his views, like everything else, are always subject to change: "I would not have any one adopt *my* mode of living on any account; for, beside that before he has fairly learned it I may have found out another for myself" (71). Thoreau is careful to give us his exact soundings of the depth of Walden Pond—102 feet—but he also tells us that it has risen 7 feet since he took that sounding (287), the clear implication being that if we want to know what its depth is right now, we will have to go out and measure it ourselves. One of the writer's chief tasks is not only to build his book but to keep it from becoming too brittle a statue. Of the notion that mortar keeps getting harder, he writes: "Such sayings themselves grow harder and adhere more firmly with age, and it would take many blows with a trowel to clean an old wiseacre of them" (241).

If the present volume, then, is a "Reader's Guide," it can be such only in the sense of Robert Frost's guide in "Directive," one "who only has at heart your getting lost" and later hopes "you're lost enough to find yourself," one of this poem's many direct echoes of *Walden*. A commentator cannot take Thoreau's most quoted advice—"Simplify, simplify" (91)—because, as critics have pointed out, Thoreau did not take it himself in composing *Walden*; why, for example, does he say it twice, and after he has just said "Simplicity, simplicity, simplicity!"? As some of you know, those little pamphlets that call themselves "Notes" claim to give you the essence of a famous literary work, sometimes without your even having to read it yourself. What they really do is take sometimes eccentric, sometimes bizarre, usually sub- versive works and domesticate them, and translate them into innocuous commonplaces and great, universal Themes. To be fair, many of our more respectable textbooks, lectures, and even professional books and articles do the same.

The rest of this book is based on a series of close readings, because such an approach gets us nearest to the life of the text. Although I necessarily present you with my own readings, this strategy brings you closest to the evidence yourself; you can immediately weigh your reading of a sentence or paragraph against mine, or be provoked to further readings of your own. *Walden*'s own words are here given the same kind of ontological privilege that concrete physical reality is given in the world of the book. Any abstractions or generalizations are suspect, or at least must be constantly measured against these sets of specifics. This book will serve its fullest purpose if you do not believe a word of it—that is, if you take every statement as only a hypothesis to measure against your own experience of reading—for this commentary on *Walden*, and even ultimately *Walden* itself, is ultimately disposable, secondary to your own living acts of thinking and feeling.

5

Structurings
The Form of Flow

When we talk about the "structure" or "form" of a book, we should be aware that we are speaking in metaphors, that we are using spatial analogies to describe an activity that exists primarily in time, for our initial encounter with the book is necessarily word by word, line by line, page by page. This sequential and temporal nature of reading has led some recent literary theorists to urge that we drop the spatial metaphors entirely, since they distort or falsify our actual experience in favor of formulations we make after that experience. But if we examine that experience carefully, we can see that as we read from moment to moment we are also seeking and creating overall patterns, connecting what we are now encountering with what we already know and with what we expect to follow. Indeed, without this constant structuring we would probably be unable to read an entire book. It is a process in which memory and anticipation are at least as crucial as immediate apprehension.

This issue of structuring is particularly important to the reading of *Walden* because the book does not clearly follow forms with which we are already familiar. Although *Walden* is not as strange to us as it was to its first readers, few as they were, it is not a novel, a narrative poem, a play. There is no clear story line or plot development, and those looking for such will inevitably be frustrated. They will treat the gist of the book as mere "setting" or "description" and will always be waiting for some dramatic action, as for "the Visitor who never comes" (270) in Hindu scripture, mentioned at the end of "Winter Visitors." In reading as in our lives themselves, we anticipate some great crisis that will change everything, missing the small but genuine drama of each passing instant, "the bloom of the present moment" (111).

Sometimes the history of how previous literary critics have responded to a problem is instructive, if only to suggest which answers are too narrow or too pat. Several earlier critics felt that Thoreau's particular genius lay in his ability to craft wonderful sentences or, at most, paragraphs. This judgment is implicit in Emerson's famous essay, based on the eulogy he delivered at Thoreau's funeral in 1862 and published that same year in the *Atlantic Monthly*. Emerson talks about Thoreau leaving his major task unfinished and mentions *Walden* itself only once and offhandedly. As examples of Thoreau's genius we are given generous samples of self-contained, aphoristic sentences, extracted primarily from the unpublished journals. This sense of a fine worker in miniatures was elaborated so eloquently in an 1865 critique by James Russell Lowell that it remained a truism of Thoreau criticism for long after:

> He had no artistic power such as controls a great work to the serene balance of completeness, but exquisite mechanical skill in the shaping of sentences and paragraphs, or (more rarely) short bits of verse for the expression of a detached thought, sentiment, or image. His works give one the feeling of a sky full of stars,—something impressive and exhilarating certainly, something high overhead and freckled thickly with spots of isolated brightness; but whether these have any mutual relations with each other, or have any concern with our mundane matters, is for the most part matter of conjecture,— astrology as yet, and not astronomy.[1]

Later, when Odell Shepard did on a larger scale what Emerson had begun—combing the journals for nuggets and set pieces—and published them in 1926 as a single volume titled *The Heart of Thoreau's Journals*, he justified this procedure by arguing that Thoreau is "habitually sententious, that his style depends very little upon construction and almost entirely upon the terse and close-grit apothegm. . . . [H]e never masters 'the art of the whole.' For better and for worse, he is essentially a *pensée* writer and not a builder of books."[2]

To the extent that Shepard seems to have arrived at this judgment himself, it may well have been from his working closely with the journals, from which standpoint the books may indeed seem cobbled together out of sentences written at first in widely different contexts. What had yet to be done, though, was a detailed analysis of *Walden* as it stood, and such an analysis F. O. Matthiessen performed in his *American Renaissance*. In a key chapter, "*Walden*: Craftmanship vs. Technique," he argues for the "structural wholeness" (Matthiessen, 173) of the book by introducing a phrase and a concept from Coleridge, that of "organic form," defined by Coleridge as "innate; it shapes as it develops, itself from within, and the fulness of its development is one and the same with the perfection of its outward form" (Matthiessen, 134). In other words, the material itself determines the form of the book in ways similar to those described by Thoreau in his discussion of architecture: "What of architectural beauty I now see, I know has gradually grown from within outward, out of the necessities and character of the indweller, who is the only builder,—out of some unconscious truthfulness, and nobleness, without ever a thought for the appearance" (47). Matthiessen's analysis was exceptional in its conciseness (the analysis itself takes up fewer than three pages), its specificity, and its elegance. He points out Thoreau's use of transitions and links between chapters, the contrasting opposites in the first half and the more seasonal progression in the second half.

As in the study of so much else in American romanticism, Matthiessen's work laid out the main lines of inquiry for at least a generation after him. R. P. Adams, writing in 1952 about more general shifts from neoclassicism to romanticism, extends the notion of "organic form" from the relation between the whole and the parts, the material and the structure, to the subject matter itself. *Walden* is "organic" because "the pattern of symbolic death and rebirth is used to express a revolt against static mechanism in favor of dynamic organicism."[3] The book-length studies of Sherman Paul[4] and Charles Anderson (Anderson, 228–57) view *Walden* as "organic" primarily because of the cycle of seasons and its related imagery. Lauriat Lane, Jr., sees "The Organic Structure of *Walden*" as consisting of five arrangements: "absolute form," "narrative movement," "expository order," "the rhetorical," and "the mythic,"[5] putting some strain on the notion of a harmonic unity. Although all these critics provide insight into the book and make previously unseen connections among its parts, the entire notion of organic form became too vague and automatic, a critical commonplace that served to stop further examination of the structure. As often happens, what is originally an iconoclastic and revisionary idea becomes itself orthodox.

One of the things the phrase "organic form" filtered out was many readers' experience of the book as asymmetrical and self-contradictory, of being constantly kept off balance. Although the arguments for organic form were often convincing, they just as often showed how well their own summaries of the chapters, rather than the chapters themselves, fit together; the arguments do not make the reading experience itself click into place together as it does with such works as *The Scarlet Letter* and *Four Quartets*. Partly in response to this aspect of reading *Walden*, and partly from what Jonathan Culler has called the principle of plenitude in literary criticism,[6] in which any position that can be taken will be taken, three pieces challenging the organic position appeared in the 1970s. I published an article in which I noted gaps and sudden juxtapositions between the literal and the symbolic and saw the meaning of the work not in some ultimate reconciliation but in the juxtapositions themselves.[7] In *Thoreau as Romantic Naturalist: His Shifting Stance toward Nature* James McIntosh traced, as his subtitle suggests, attitudes within *Walden* that are never resolved or synthesized.[8] Two years later, Walter Benn Michaels, who seems not to have read these two other works, published "*Walden*'s False Bottoms," in which he argues that Thoreau keeps implying some kind of solid foundation for reality, such as "nature," but is always pulling it out from under us.[9] Although the three readings, taken together, seem to be a throwback to the views of Lowell, the important difference is that they tend to see the lack of unity and coherence less as the result of artistic inabilities than as deliberate strategies by the author; they take with some literalness Thoreau's statement that he is following the bent of his genius, "which is a very crooked one" (56).

The challenge to criticism now is not so much to directly resolve the debate about *Walden*'s unity but to ask how this single text can underwrite such opposing points of view. Is the book an intricate but intertwined spiderweb, as Charles Anderson maintains, or is it more like a kaleidoscope or a fun-house hall of mirrors? As we read and analyze, should we focus more on the similarities between images in various parts of the book, or on how they differ from one another in each context? What is the best way for a reading like this to proceed—chapter by chapter in a more temporal way, or topic by topic? Should we give the reader a road map or abandon him or her to a labyrinthine reading experience?

A partial answer to the first question lies in the history of critical assumptions and tastes. Matthiessen wrote in the midst of what was then, and to some extent is still, called the New Criticism. There was something of a consensus that unity, coherence, and achieved form were intrinsic to literary greatness. Although Matthiessen himself did not work within many of the limitations the New Critics imposed on themselves—a deliberate isolating of the work from its historical and political contexts, an intentional black-boxing of the text from an author's intentions and its reader's reactions—he shared the New Critics' concerns and methods about aesthetic form and quality. While he would never have approved of the ways later critics would use these methods to blunt Thoreau's social visions, his own analysis gave them the tools to do so.

When McIntosh, Michaels, and I wrote these analyses, the climate of New Critical assumptions was still predominant, but those assumptions were coming to be viewed as just that—assumptions, not eternal truths about art. New theories from the Continent were being studied, theories that stressed the slipperiness and contradictory aspects of all writing. Any final unity or total "meaning" of a text was seen as imposed rather than elicited. Most important, though, New Criticism was turning from a vision to simply a method, a way to crank out readings. Yet this shift in critical emphasis is not a complete explanation. Other works have not undergone such wide swings in the ways their structure is perceived; nor do their structures now seem so unresolved and enigmatic.

Returning to the questions, my tentative answers lie more in the nature of the text and in its writing. The disagreements between critics reflect tensions in the book itself; each side accurately portrays one of the two vectors involved, a struggle for unity, for relating all parts of experience, and an equal distrust of any kind of unity or resolution. These two pulls can be viewed in terms of the opposition described at the beginning of this chapter: the reader's desire to build a larger whole from the book and the sometimes conflicting or spoiling experience of reading each separate word and sentence. The text itself is always moving toward structuring itself, yet always pulling back from doing so. What is a problem for both writer and reader becomes a major issue in the book itself, which, as we have seen, is concerned with its own writing from the first sentence on.

To pursue this matter further, we should look in detail at some of the relevant passages in the *Journal* and in *Walden*. On the one hand, Thoreau felt that the crafted work of art creates something of permanent value, something that can preserve, enrich, and even transmute life. But on the other hand, he found that the act of structuring art can freeze and atrophy the very flow of life he treasured. The more positive values of the work of art can be heard in an early journal meditation on a Native American stone implement: "The Indian must have possessed no small share of vital energy—to have rubbed industriously stone upon stone for long months, till at length he had rubbed out an axe or pestle— As though he had said in the face of the constant flux of things—I at least will live an enduring life" (*Journal*, 1:39). Later Thoreau refers to the arrowheads he finds as "stone fruit" that carry traces of their creators' selves into the future, "mindprints," instead of "footprints," physical tracks of mental motions (*Journal*, XII:90–91).

In *Walden*, the positive side of the artist being able to intensify and even transcend time is most famously rendered in a parable about another artifact by another kind of Indian:

> There was an artist in the city of Kouroo who was disposed to strive after perfection. One day it came into his mind to make a staff. Having considered that in an imperfect work time is an ingredient, but into a perfect work time does not enter, he said to himself, It shall be perfect in all respects, though I should do nothing else in my life. He proceeded instantly to the forest for wood, being resolved that it should not be made of unsuitable material; and as he searched for and rejected stick after stick, his friends gradually deserted him, for they grew old in their works and died, but he grew not older by a moment. . . . By the time he had smoothed and polished the staff Kalpa was no longer the pole-star; and ere he had put on the ferrule and the head adorned with precious stones, Brahma had awoke and slumbered many times. But why do I stay to mention these things? When the finishing stroke was put to his work, it suddenly expanded before the eyes of the astonished artist into the fairest of all the creations of Brahma.
>
> (326–27)

Reading this passage as an analogue to the writing of *Walden* has become another critical cliché. But what comes clearly through the passage is the sense of quiet joy, of the irrepressible satisfaction from deliberate, careful, all-absorbing crafting, an uncompromising quest that proceeds step by step but reaches a sudden culmination. Yet even in this rhapsodic appreciation of the possibilities of art, one can hear a more divided attitude, a melancholy undercurrent, especially in words like "his friends gradually deserted him, for they grew old in their works and died." We remember here that Henry's first book was written as a memorial to his brother John, in some ways a substitute for that close friendship, and that the years writing *Walden* also saw the ebbing of Thoreau's personal relationship with Emerson.

While the passage seems to move toward a state of eternity, it is oddly interrupted by a question—"But why do I stay to mention these things?"—that returns the focus to a speaker setting down words in time—"When I wrote the following pages"—the element that seems to be denied or transcended. Further, this eternity can be conceived and measured only in temporal units—the deaths of friends, cycles of sleep and waking, the shifting of the earth's axis to create changes in the North Star, that symbol of constancy. The key word in this undercurrent is "astonished," for in its etymology it means turned to stone. As discussed more extensively in the next chapter, Thoreau was always aware of the roots of the words he used, and often borrowed resonances from these roots. Here he could draw on the roots of the word as Emerson had already done in his 1842 poem "The Snow-storm," in which the north wind

> Leaves, when the sun appears, astonished Art
> To mimic in slow structures, stone by stone,
> Built in an age, the mad wind's night-work,
> The frolic architecture of the snow.[10]

Human art, in both the poem and the passage, is painfully slow, even plodding, compared with natural creation. The stones in the poem are like commemorative statues that mark only the once living presence but not living thought itself.

And so the artifact—the sculpted stone ax and even the staff—can be viewed more negatively as a dead monument bearing only an inverse relationship to the living spirit that created it. The "vital energy" is irrevocably lost, and only the still, mute stone remains. Art and life do not always exist in harmony but frequently involve painful choice. In A Week Thoreau included these awkward but clear-sighted lines: "My life has been the poem I would have writ, / But I could not both live and utter it."[11] And a few pages earlier, he complained that "it is not easy to write in a journal what interests us at any time, because to write it is not what interests us" (A Week, 322). In a journal entry written after the composition of Walden, Thoreau could still write, "The real facts of a poet's life would be of more value to us than any work of his art. I mean that the very scheme and form of his poetry (so called) is adopted at a sacrifice of vital truth and poetry"

(*Journal*, X:131). The very achievement of artistic form here seems to be at odds with the truths of life itself.

This discomfort with what writing takes away from life and with what it fails to capture from it can be traced to early journal passages, such as the following, which appears just a few pages before the passage about the stone ax: "But what does all this scribbling amount to?—What is now scribbled in the heat of the moment one can contemplate with somewhat of satisfaction, but alas! To-morrow–aye to-night— it is stale, flat—and unprofitable—in fine, is not, only its shell remains—like some red parboiled lobster-shell—which kicked aside never so often still stares at you in the path" (*Journal*, 1:33–34). The shell is not the living creature but merely a hard, external skeleton, a dead husk, somewhat like the embedded and unacknowledged words lifted from Shakespeare. This entry is an early version of the sentences quoted in chapter 4: "The volatile truth of our words should continually betray the inadequacy of the residual statement. Their truth is instantly *translated*; its literal monument alone remains" (325). As noted, "literal" is used effectively because it refers to the letters themselves, the physical building blocks, for letters are to the writer what stone is to the sculpture. Putting the letters together is the result of a process as active and artful as rubbing stone on stone; the letters, themselves, however, are only "mindprints," mere tracks that thought left passing this way but not the prey itself. Throughout *Walden*, monuments, especially stone ones, are unfavorably compared to the living presence: "Most of the stone a nation hammers goes toward its tomb only. It buries itself alive" (58); "Many are concerned about the monuments of the West and the East,—to know who built them. For my part, I should like to know who in those days did not build them" (58); and "In Arcadia, when I was there, I did not see any hammering stone" (57).

Behind the structure of *Walden* and enacted within it, then, are two competing drives, one an immediate openness to flux, a responsiveness to a continually changing world, and the other a desire to rescue and preserve from that world something of permanent shape and beauty. Thoreau's wish to somehow have both can be seen in a meditation on the central image in his first book: "A man's life should be constantly as fresh as this river. It should be the same channel, but a new water every instant" (*A Week*, 132). A worthy goal, then, would be to write a book like a river—where a perennial flux runs through a constant form. But they are not as easy to reconcile as this image suggests. When we look at a river we are usually able to focus on only one aspect of it—either the shapes created by the banks or the current of the river.

The relation of form and flux, how they do and do not relate to each other, can be seen in the juxtaposition of the third chapter, "Reading," with the fourth chapter, "Sounds." Significantly, each title reflects a different aspect of the language activity we are engaged in— "Reading" stresses the patterning of the sounds of speech into more enduring forms, and "Sounds," by contrast, stresses the immediate duration of speech, its physical, transient aspect, and embraces the nonmeaningful, even the nonhuman. More important, each chapter offers a different kind of reading experience.

Of all the chapters in the book, "Reading" is the one that reads most like a self-contained essay, perhaps an essay by Emerson. It has the smaller proportion of direct narrative and the fewest references to Thoreau's life at the pond. And indeed such references as occur are largely negative. Thoreau did not read much that first summer, since he had to finish his house and hoe his beans. He kept the *Iliad* on his table but looked at it only occasionally. The books he did read were merely the kinds of travel books he mocked in the first couple of pages, not the more lasting literature he extols here. More important, the voice here is particularly disembodied, its first sentence making no transition from what came before: "With a little more deliberation in the choice of their pursuits, all men would perhaps become essentially students and observers, for certainly their nature and destiny are interesting to all alike" (99). The diction especially is abstract and generalizing; in how many sentences, particularly sentences by Thoreau, do we see a string of words like "all men," "essentially," "certainly," "nature," "destiny," and "all alike"? The rest of the paragraph continues to reinforce this sense of eternal truth, mainly through expressions that negate time: "*im*mortal," "no change nor accident," no dust," "no time," "neither past, present, nor future" (99). One of the main arguments the chapter develops—a position demonstrated as much by its tone as by a logical succession of reasons—is how speech differs from writing precisely because the latter rises above the immediate context of "sound" and can exist in a more abstract realm that can be contemplated in cool deliberation: "there is a memorable interval between the spoken and written language, the language heard and the language read. The one is commonly transitory, a *sound*, a tongue, a dialect merely, almost brutish" (101, emphasis added).

"Sounds" begins its contrast to "Reading" immediately in its title and then in its very first word, "But," an uncommon way to begin a chapter: "But while we are confined to books, though the most select and classic, and read only particular written languages, which are themselves but dialects and provincial, we are in danger of forgetting the language which all things and events speak without metaphor, which alone is copious and standard" (111). It is sometimes difficult to recall one's first reading of a passage, but even in retrospect the reversal here strikes me as quite dramatic and complete. Similarly, other chapter openings that have been called "transitions" are almost violent in their reversals, as in the first sentence of "Visitors": "I think that I love society as much as most, and am ready enough to fasten myself like a blood-sucker for the time to any full-blooded man that comes in my way" (140). "Reading" is written with such conviction, its tone is so authoritative, that we are surprised to find it delimited here so radically and so quickly. As we have just seen, Thoreau has criticized everyday speech for being "a dialect merely," but here even the most select and classic books are written in languages "which are themselves but dialects and provincial." Through a series of puns Thoreau reminds us how small an amount of life has been captured in books: "Much is published but little printed." That is, much is already public, open to the eyes and ears of all, but very little finds its ways into books. It is "without metaphor" because the very putting into print is a kind of metaphor. Just as highly as Thoreau has praised the activity of reading, he now severely qualifies it: "No method nor discipline can supersede the necessity of being forever on the alert. What is a course of history, or philosophy, or poetry, no matter how well selected, or the best society, or the most admirable routine of life, compared with the discipline of looking always at what is to be seen? Will you be a reader, a student merely, or a seer? Read your fate, see what is before you, and walk on into futurity" (111). Thoreau puns here on the double meaning of "seer" as one who looks into the future and as one who sees: for Thoreau, the latter is rarer and more inclusive. This double meaning makes "before" take on both its spatial and its temporal meanings. We can see what is "before" us as fate if we see clearly what is right in front of us. The rest of the chapter soon moves into the present tense.

At this point I find myself asking, What is the relation of the two chapters? The rest of the book gives little help; Thoreau seems to enjoy reading and talking philosophy as much as watching squirrels. Of course, as we read, more of the world of "Sounds" becomes printed as well as published through Thoreau's writing, but this paradox does not really reconcile the two realms. A quotation from Emerson begins to help: "Literature is a point outside our hodiernal circle, through which a new one may be described. . . . In like manner, we see literature best from the midst of wild nature, or from the din of affairs, or from a high religion. The field cannot be well seen from within the field" (Emerson, 408–9). Emerson makes an appropriate metaphor through a pun, with "field" as a physical area and "field" as a discipline, a course of study. This visualization reminds us that we can see some aspects of a field—its soil, vegetation—inside it and other aspects— its shape, its limits—better outside it. This kind of perception is not just a local insight, but the structuring principle in the volume in which it appears, for Emerson's *Essays, First Series* is built around such matched pairs as "History" and "Self-Reliance," "Prudence" and "Heroism." This structure enacts Emerson's notion that opposites juxtaposed give more of the truth than any single vantage point can. We can see the juxtaposition of "Reading" and "Sounds" in light of the following sentence from Emerson: "But it is the fault of our rhetoric that we cannot strongly state one fact without seeming to belie some other" (Emerson, 255–56). This strategy also helps explain the otherwise anomalous appearance of the "Complemental Verses" after the first long chapter (80)—a quotation inserted not to support or amplify a text but, rather, to disagree with or qualify it. It provides literally another voice from that of the author, asking the reader to consider also the obverse of everything just said.

We can see some of these notions at work in the entirety of *Walden* from the table of contents:

1. Economy
2. Where I Lived, and What I Lived For
3. Reading
4. Sounds
5. Solitude
6. Visitors
7. The Bean-Field
8. The Village
9. The Ponds
10. Baker Farm
11. Higher Laws
12. Brute Neighbors
13. House-Warming
14. Former Inhabitants; and Winter Visitors
15. Winter Animals
16. The Pond in Winter
17. Spring
18. Conclusion

The paired contrasts are particularly obvious through the first 12 chapters: "Economy" implies the workings of an entire culture, while "Where I Lived" suggests a more personal alternative; the pairing of "Solitude," and "Visitors," like that of "The Bean-Field" and "The Village," suggests a further contrast between the individualistic and the communal; the purity of "The Ponds" contrasts with what Thoreau sees as the self-imposed squalor of the Fields family living on "Baker Farm"; and whereas "Higher Laws" beseeches us to rise above nature, "Brute Neighbors" immerses us in it. Thus, a pattern seems to emerge, with paired opposites clustered around such roughly parallel dualisms as society versus the individual, culture versus nature, and complexity versus simplicity.

Some such delineation finds its way into almost every discussion of *Walden*'s structure. But we must ask what is left here, what is not accounted for, and why this pairing is even less clear after chapter 12. The critical strategy, already noted, of making capsule summaries of each chapter and then fitting the capsules together has been too easily accepted, for the chapters themselves contain diverse, sometimes conflicting material. For example, the two readings I have given of "Reading" in this chapter and the preceding are very different from each other, not through any deception but only through my selecting different sentences in each case to quote and analyze. The entire book is much more complex than it will appear to be from any reading, this one included.

To proceed with our antistructuring examination of the structure, then, "Economy" includes a good deal about Thoreau's personal values, about how and why he built his hut in the woods, just as "Where I Lived, and What I Lived For" contains long passages of social criticism—about newspapers and railroad building, for example—that would be just as appropriate for the preceding chapter. Though we have seen how much "Reading" and "Sounds" contrast with each other, as we look more closely we can see how much their textures interpenetrate. One of the main ways of praising classics is through the imagery of nature—for example, "We might as well omit to study Nature because she is old" (100); these books "were first written on bark" (99) and take on through the years "only a maturer golden and autumnal tint" (102). Conversely, much of "Sounds" is rendered in literary terms: the torn sails Thoreau sees in this chapter on a railroad car are "proof-sheets which need no correction" (119); the screech owls are "truly Ben Jonsonian" (124); the bullfrogs trump "in their Stygian lake,—if the Walden nymphs will pardon the comparison" (126). Even though the two chapters are presented as opposites, each is also used as a metaphor for the other, suggesting subterranean connections.

Similarly, the second paragraph of "Solitude" is actually about visitors to the small house in the woods, or at least the traces they leave behind. This short but memorable passage brings to mind the Oriental yin-yang symbol of complementary opposites—wherein a small spot of light is in the dark section and a small spot of dark is in the light section—for this small preview of the next chapter, "Visitors," gives a greater clarity and contrast to "Solitude." The second paragraph of "The Bean-Field," like the third paragraph of "The Ponds," plays with the irony that what is now Thoreau's home was once the end point of journeys he took from home. Both sections serve to make these demarcations of contrasting areas more fluid, more dependent on shifts in time and perspective than on any inherent qualities. And we know from the first paragraph that Thoreau is "at present . . . a sojourner in civilized life again" (3), and so the perspective has shifted yet one more time. Further, as Thoreau works in the field he cannot help but be reminded of the attitudes and doings of the village, for he hears the comments of travelers on the road and the sound of guns, both celebrating what is said to be our liberty and training to extend that liberty to Mexican-held territories.

"The Ponds" and "Baker Farm" are two chapters often cited as contrasts, but pointed out less often is how each contains within it its own set of contrasts. Thoreau's own stance toward the ponds is contrasted within that chapter with a long diatribe against the grasping, eponymous owner of Flint's Pond, one of whose mistakes was to have refused Thoreau permission to live by it. The visit to Baker Farm is framed within its chapter by passages describing the walk there and back, embracing the carefree, exuberant life in nature that Thoreau lives. And the famous scene of Thoreau's glimpsing a woodchuck and being seized with a desire to eat it raw occurs in a chapter titled "Higher Laws." Thus, while the structurings of polarity are clear as we look at chapter headings, it is easy to see that these polar opposites operate within each chapter as well as between them.

Almost as clear, as we look at the chapter headings, is the cycle of the seasons. Although critics differ as to where the cycle begins— some see the beginning in spring, when Thoreau describes cutting down trees for his house; others, in summer, when the first detailed accounts of life at the pond begin—all have noticed the pattern itself. Within that pattern of the seasonal cycles are linked chapters of smaller natural cycles, for as Thoreau says, "the day is an epitome of the year" (301). "Sounds," for example, can be said to begin on either a summer morning or a summer afternoon but definitely ends at dawn the next day, just as the book itself ends at the beginning of spring. And just as the structuring of opposites is more predominant in the first half of the book, the seasonal arrangement is more so in the second half, and the modes of writing change accordingly. Whereas in the first half the chapters are more topically arranged and essaylike, in the second half description and narrative arrangements are more predominant; even when episodes have clear social messages, as does "Baker Farm," those criticisms are framed in descriptive and narrative terms.

What is the significance of this shift, and can we view it as part of a larger structuring that relates the two halves of the book? As we have seen, critics who have studied the book's development in genetic terms, as a process of composition occurring over several years, see the change as reflecting Thoreau's altering focus, from outward to inward, from social to psychological and naturalistic. But what meanings does this shift have for the reader who deals with the book in terms of days or weeks rather than years? The suggestion I make here depends on what came to be a tradition of symbolism among American, particularly New England, writers, but that began to be self-conscious only in its later stages. From the earliest accounts of explorers and settlers the contrasts of the New England climate were noted and recorded, often assuming symbolic values, as, say, a kind of purgation that God required of his chosen people.

Henry Adams, writing at the transition between the nineteenth and twentieth centuries, uses this symbology extensively and explicitly as he recounts his own early years, spending the winters in Boston and the summers in the more rural seaside town of Quincy: "From earliest childhood the boy was accustomed to feel that for him life was double. Winter and summer, town and country, law and liberty were hostile."[12] One senses that the parallels between these paired opposites of time, space, and abstractions are more than literary metaphors; they are also inherent in the very act of coming to consciousness in such a situation. As Adams writes, "The chief charm of New England was harshness of contrasts and extremes of sensibility—a cold that froze the blood, and a heat that boiled it. . . . The violence of the contrast was real and made the strongest motive of education. The double exterior nature gave life its relative values. Winter and summer, cold and heat, town and country, force and freedom, marked two modes of life and thought, balanced like lobes of the brain" (Adams, 727). What saves these contrasts from melodrama is the undertone of Yankee humor and irony, as when weather that in turn freezes and boils the blood is described as "the chief charm of New England." But for Adams, writing in a world he experienced as increasingly chaotic and entropic, these opposites were ultimately "irreconcilable problems, irreducible opposites" (Adams, 728).

Thoreau, however, had faith—although not blind or easy—that the relation between seasons and other contraries need not be simply one of opposition. Perhaps if one were able to catch that very moment of transition when winter turned into spring, one could discover something of the usually occulted relations between the two, trace what exactly continued as well as what changed. As Thoreau says in what I consider one of the key sentences in the book, "Every incident connected with the breaking up of the rivers and ponds and the settling of the weather is particularly interesting to us who live in a climate of so great extremes" (303). The climax of *Walden* is not simply spring but the very movement from winter to spring. In a paragraph before the sentence just quoted, Thoreau says, "One attraction in coming to the woods to live was that I should have leisure and opportunity to see the spring come in" (302). The particular phrasing of not simply seeing the spring but seeing it *come in* is as deliberate as everything else in the book. In one of the few times he repeats even a phrase, Thoreau uses the same expression in discussing his imaginative possession of house sites, describing the act of living in terms of passing through seasons: "Well, there I might live, I said; and there I did live, for an hour, a summer and a winter life; saw how I could let the years run off, buffet the winter through, and see the spring come in" (81). In one of the great understatements of the book, Thoreau says, "I am on the alert for the first signs of spring" (302).

For Thoreau even more than for Adams, the cycle of the seasons was not simply a literary convention; as he grew older, and particularly during the nine years *Walden* was being written, he came to feel that answers to philosophical or even theological questions could come from close, systematic observations of nature. He says in one journal entry, "The process that goes on in the sod and the dark, about the minute fibres of the grass,—the chemistry and the mechanics,—before a single green blade can appear above the withered herbage, if it could [be] adequately described, would supplant all other revelations" (*Journal*, V:69). And this concern with transitions between seasons was lifelong for Thoreau. Even in his earliest writing, "The Seasons," a conventional schoolboy theme, he describes the spring in terms of the passing winter: "Now we see the ice beginning to thaw, and the trees to bud."[13] In his first published nature essay in the *Dial*, he writes, "If there were no other vicissitudes than the seasons, our interest would never tire."[14] Early in Thoreau's life, this interest was associated with the idea of going to live by a pond, as an entry from 1841, four years before he moved out to Walden Pond indicates: "I want to go soon and live away by the pond where I shall hear only the wind whispering among the reeds. . . . But my friends ask what I will do when I get there? Will it not be employment enough to watch the progress of the seasons?" (*Journal*, 1:347).

The promise of the second half of the book is that the divisions bifurcating our lives have some chance of reconciliation. This view not only helps link together the two halves but also helps explain other anomalies. For instance, some debate has arisen as to whether "House-Warming" is a fall or winter chapter.[15] But read in the context just suggested, it is more clearly about the transition between fall and winter. With its lists of dates about the freezing of the ice, the movement of the Walden water from flux to fixity, "House-Warming" is a companion piece to "Spring," with its descriptions of thawing and its lists of dates of the pond's opening. Just as in "Spring" Thoreau is concerned with the first intimations of the coming season, in "House-

Warming" he tries to catch the first signs of winter's onset: "Already, by the first of September, I had seen two or three small maples turned scarlet across the pond, beneath where the white stems of three aspens diverged, at the point of a promontory, next the water. Ah, many a tale their color told!" (239–40). And just as in "Spring" he is concerned about what of winter persists in spring—"it was pleasant to compare the first tender signs of the infant year just peeping forth with stately beauty of the withered vegetation which had withstood the winter" (309)—in "House-Warming" he tracks the persistence of summer in fall: "I thus warmed myself by the still glowing embers which the summer, like a departed hunter, had left" (240).

This view also helps us understand chapters like "The Village." As we look carefully at this, the shortest chapter in the book, we see that more space is taken up by the traveling between the village and the pond than by words about either site. As with Emerson's field, each can best be seen from the vantage of the other—or, even better, from a point outside both, in the passage between the two. Significantly, what most critics see as the major epiphany in the book—the meditation on thawing clay—happens neither at the pond nor in the village but in transition between them.

Walden, then, is a book concerned with transitions, with passage, as its first paragraph seems to warn us. Its author wished to toe the line not only between the past and the future but also between all dualities, since for him that boundary gives the fullest perspective. The book is an enactment in experiential and concrete terms of Emerson's statement "Power ceases in the instant of repose; it resides in the moment of transition from a past to a new state, in the shooting of a gulf, in the darting to an aim" (Emerson, 271) and, more elaborately, "Our strength is transitional, alternating; or, shall I say, a thread of two strands. The sea-shore, sea seen from shore, shore seen from sea; the taste of two metals in contact. . . . the experience of poetic creativeness, which is not found in staying at home, nor yet in travelling, but in transitions from one to the other, which must therefore be adroitly managed to present as much transitional surface as possible" (Emerson, 641).

One thematic thread that is resolved through this stress on transitions is the tension between form and flux with which we began this chapter. We see Thoreau coming to an appreciation of certain kinds of aesthetic experiences that capture the fluidity of life in some sort of framing or form. It is in the transition of his house from an unfinished to a finished form that he notices the advantages of each and particularly comes to treasure the play of shadows: "My house never pleased my eye so much after it was plastered, though I was obliged to confess that it was more comfortable. Should not every apartment in which man dwells be lofty enough to create some obscurity over-head, where flickering shadows may play at evening about the rafters? These forms are more agreeable to the fancy and imagination than fresco paintings or other the most expensive furniture" (242). Fresco paintings, of course, remain the same except when they fade, whereas the "forms" the fire creates are always changing, flickering. The obscurity creates a certain margin for interpretation, for imagination. Thoreau says of his own writing, "I do not suppose that I have obtained to obscurity, but I should be proud if no more fatal fault were found with my pages" (325). But this obscurity coexists with a clarity of outline and with sharp contrasts between light and dark. In a similar spirit Thoreau praises the movements of thawing clay on a railroad embankment: "You may melt your metals and cast them into the most beautiful moulds you can; they will never excite me like the forms which this molten earth flows out into" (309). There are several kinds of echoings here, such as "melt," "metals," "moulds," and "molten," but the most important juxtaposition is "forms" and "flows." Indeed, in this five-page passage both of these words are used more often than in the rest of the book combined. The metals, like the frescoes, harden permanently into immutable shapes, while the clay flows and still retains some kind of form. The tension can be traced in the following sentence: "It is wonderful how rapidly yet perfectly the sand organizes itself as it flows, using the best material its mass affords to form the sharp edges of its channel" (307). Here is movement, but organized movement; here are sharply defined edges, but the edges are never static. We can see Thoreau trying to reformulate this more metamorphic sense of form by ringing some changes on the various forms of "form":

"When the flowing mass reaches the drain at the foot of the bank it spreads out flatter into *strands*, the separate streams losing their semi-cylindrical form and gradually becoming more flat and broad, running together as they are moist, till they form an almost flat *sand*, still variously and beautifully shaded, but in which you can trace the original forms of vegetation; till at length, in the water itself, they are converted into *banks*, like those formed off the mouths of rivers, and the forms of vegetation are lost in the ripple marks on the bottom" (305). Both the flickering shadows and the thawing clay are emblems of the kind of art form *Walden* aspires to be, one that retains a certain clarity of outline, yet also a kind of unfinished openness.

It has by now become a tradition of *Walden* criticism to note how traditional it is to write a book patterned on the cycle of the seasons. What Thoreau has done, though, is to set his book on the cusps between the seasons, to search for that point in time before opposites bifurcate and to publish to the world its secrets of flux, complementarity, and transition. Emerson wrote, "Our moods do not believe in each other" (Emerson, 406), and Thoreau, anticipating Henry Adams, noted, "We really have four seasons, each incredible to the other" (*Journal*, III:233). The structurings of *Walden* affirm, though, that there are moments—moments that, with patience, receptivity, and luck, we can perceive—before spirit and matter, life and death, childhood and adulthood, flux and form split apart from each other, moments when they are not only credible to each other but embrace each other as well.

6

Languages
Root Meanings

We have seen how the estimates of Thoreau as a great stylist whose genius flourished primarily in the small arenas of sentence and paragraph obscured his achievements in the larger structurings of *Walden*. More surprising is that this same reputation has also prevented us from seeing some of what Thoreau is actually doing at these levels of writing and how this factor relates to those structurings. A journal entry by Emerson is the first instance of what has become the conventional wisdom about the relation between the two writers: "I told H.T. that his freedom is in the form, but he does not disclose new matter. I am very familiar with all his thoughts—they are my own quite originally drest."[1] The author of a dissertation on the development of Thoreau's style writes of *Walden*, "Thoreau had to give little thought to what he wanted to say and devoted most of his time to revising sentences and paragraphs in expression and order."[2] Whether the ideas were originally Emerson's or already settled and unproblematic in Thoreau's own mind, the presumption here is that Thoreau's distinction lies in just presenting them or dressing them up. And yet if there is one principle the various schools of literary criticism agree on, it is the primacy of language, the sense that content cannot be neatly abstracted from style, that the medium to a large extent is the message. Even if Thoreau deliberately set out to express Emerson's philosophy in a more concrete language, that philosophy would inevitably be changed in the course of its expression.

But like everything that has become conventional wisdom, this view of Thoreau translating Emerson into specificity has some truth in it, and I think that truth might best be expressed as follows. Thoreau became the writer he did in good part by first accepting and then building on and extending Emerson's own notions of language. That is, Thoreau became a better prose writer than Emerson, just as Whitman became a greater poet than Emerson, by following even further lines Emerson had laid out. If Thoreau used more specific language than his mentor did, it must be acknowledged that he was primarily following his mentor's advice in so doing. And while several recent studies have shown Thoreau's deep interest in the language theories of his day, anything he found of use was related to ways of thinking about language that are basically Emersonian. To paraphrase T. S. Eliot, Thoreau came to know more than Emerson about language, but only because Emerson was such a central part of what Thoreau knew.

An analysis of *Walden*'s language or style should not, then, be a catalog of devices but a demonstration of how the writing embodies the vision of the book and vice versa. In an elementary way, there is nothing in the book that is not language, except perhaps the map of Walden Pond that Thoreau drew himself and had inserted in "The Ponds in Winter" chapter. Anything we have to say about imagery, ethics, psychology, or philosophy comes to us through the medium of words. This is the reason that in this volume there is much close analysis of language in every chapter, not just the present one. The volatile truths of *Walden* exist not beyond or behind its language in a Platonic realm of ideas, but, rather, only in our encounter with its words.

We can begin to trace this relation between words and vision with Emerson's first book, *Nature*, which Thoreau read in 1837, his senior year in college. The section called "Language" begins with three related propositions:

1. Words are signs of natural facts.
2. Particular natural facts are symbols of particular spiritual facts.
3. Nature is the symbol of spirit. (Emerson, 20)

In explaining the first proposition, Emerson maintains that all language, no matter how abstract or "spiritual" it is now, was once specific, sensuous in that its first use arose from an impression made on at least one of the senses. "Every word which is used to express a moral or intellectual fact, if traced to its root, is found to be borrowed from some material appearance" (Emerson, 20). Tracing language back to its origins in physical reality is particularly important, because as the second proposition suggests, these "natural facts" are inherently meaningful in that they indicate spiritual facts. And as the third proposition says, all natural facts have both their origin and their ultimate meaning in spirit or mind, not in a separate God but in a consciousness that we all potentially share.

Emerson's formulations were compelling in his time because they joined a basically Lockean theory of mind and language to a total cosmology that was monistic and idealistic. Although later American writers, Thoreau included, came to be skeptical about the metaphysics, what they took from Emerson was a set of dispositions about language and composing. Probably the central one was a kind of linguistic primitivism, a sense that simpler, less "civilized" people spoke a language that in its deepest sense was more authentic, closer to some kind of primary truth. In light of this idea, Thoreau's move out to Walden, his building of a house, and his working in nature were not mainly to get the leisure to write or even mainly to live more in accord with certain values, but, rather, to return to a condition in which language is at once truer and more poetic, there being from this Emersonian perspective no difference between the two. Thoreau tells us in "The Bean-Field," for example, the real reason he hoed beans: "Not that I wanted beans to eat, for I am by nature a Pythagorean, so far as beans are concerned, whether they mean porridge or voting, and exchanged them for rice; but, perchance, as some must work in fields if only for the sake of tropes and expression, to serve a parable-maker one day" (162).

Languages

From the Emersonian point of view, all nature is a parable of the spirit, and so God himself could be the "parable-maker." But if we focus on the root meaning of "parable," the notion of "speech" is unearthed. The parable maker is Thoreau, the writer or poet who in another mode will convert experience into truth, not only by telling us tales but by refreshing the medium of language itself. He works out here on the very boundary between the wild and the cultivated, constantly turning the former into the latter with both hoe and pen.

To explore further how Emersonian notions of language have been assimilated and extended by Thoreau, we can look at a passage from "House-Warming":

> It would seem as if the very language of our parlors would lose all its nerve and degenerate into *palaver* wholly, our lives pass at such remoteness from its symbols, and its metaphors and tropes are necessarily so far fetched, through slides and dumb-waiters, as it were; in other words, the parlor is so far from the kitchen and workshop. The dinner even is only the parable of a dinner, commonly. As if only the savage dwelt near enough to Nature and Truth to borrow a trope from them. How can the scholar, who dwells away in the North West Territory or the Isle of Man, tell what is parliamentary in the kitchen?
>
> (244–45)

This passage comes immediately after Thoreau's countervision of a huge, primitive house that is all one great hall, where one can see plainly and simultaneously its construction, the other inhabitants, and the household tasks, such as washing and cooking. Here, by contrast, we see the results of the increasing compartmentalization of our activities and our vocabularies. The "parlor," fulfilling its etymology, becomes a realm of speech only—dull, polite chatter, or "palaver"— because we disconnect it from our physical work, where speech should actually be created. This wordplay also sensitizes us to the same root puns in "parable," which we have just seen in the bean-field passage, and in "parliamentary."

The processes by which living in the world is turned into language are hidden from us by walls of misplaced propriety and a self-defeating division of labor. "Dumb-waiters" suggests not only a kind of auto-matic, mechanical servitude but also a muteness and even stupidity imposed on what or who should be doing the speaking. The dinner, appearing mysteriously through this dumb-waiter, is described and discussed in self-contained parlor language by those to whom its prepa-ration and even its immediate physical reality have become distant. We end up eating our own words. The scholar, unlike Emerson's "American Scholar," is trapped in a web of his own spinning, of other documents and books written by other scholars, and so becomes stranded on the Isle of Man, on these solely human, constricting verbal constructions. In our isolation we seek some mythical Northwest Pas-sage, without realizing that the way out is simply the immediate appre-hension of our own lives.

What this section tracks is a kind of linguistic entropy, a continual process by which, through laziness, overrefinement, or just the attrition of time, language loses touch with the physicality from which it arose. Or, to borrow a trope from Emerson, the language becomes fossilized, its original poetry lost to abstraction and habit. As he writes in *Nature*,

> New imagery ceases to be created, and old words are perverted to stand for things which are not; a paper currency is employed, when there is no bullion in the vaults. In due time, the fraud is manifest, and words lose all power to stimulate the understanding or the affections. Hundreds of writers may be found in every long-civilized nation, who for a short time believe, and make others believe, that they see and utter truths, who do not of themselves clothe one thought in its natural garment, but who feed unconsciously on the language created by the primary writers of the country, those, namely, who hold primarily on nature. But wise men pierce this rotten diction and fasten words again to visible things.
>
> —Emerson, 22–23

At the risk of perpetuating the very simplicities I warned against, we can see how thoroughly Thoreau took this stance and made it his own:

> He would be a poet who could impress the winds and streams into his service, to speak for him; who nailed words to their primitive

senses, as farmers drive down stakes in the spring, which the frost
has heaved; who derived his words as often as he used them—
transplanted them to his page with earth adhering to their roots;
whose words were so true and fresh and natural that they would
appear to expand like the buds at the approach of spring, though
they lay half smothered between two musty leaves in a library—
aye, to bloom and bear fruit there, after their kind, annually, for
the faithful reader, in sympathy with surrounding nature.

—*Natural*, 120

Thoreau's version does not just fasten words to "visible" things but
uses other senses, such as smell ("musty"), the tactile sensations of
nailing (through accented monosyllables like "drive down stakes"),
and blooming. A physical heft is added to buried metaphors, such as
the "roots"—with earth still adhering—of both plants and words, or
the "leaves" of both nature and books.

But even in this effective passage one is tempted to say "Easier
said than done." How can one pierce rotten diction without creating
a whole new language? How can one make an auroral hut out of a
run-down shanty? We can begin to answer such questions by focusing
on Thoreau's use of "far fetched" in the parlor passage. What has
happened here is that in our ordinary usage the two words in the
phrase have become yoked so that we no longer hear or see them
separately. We take the entire phrase as a single word, a synonym for
extreme, even ridiculous. But Thoreau, bringing our sensory imagination into play, recontextualizes the expression, fastens words again to
visible things, by having our metaphors fetched through actual space,
"through slides and dumb-waiters."

This fossil poetry resides not so much in just the physical meaning,
as might be assumed from reading only Emerson's formulation, as in
the simultaneous holding of both the literal and the figurative meaning—a point Thoreau was often clearer about. Indeed, this holding
together could be said to define metaphoric or poetic language, for
metaphors or similes are most effective not when they link just any
two things, no matter how appropriate, but when they use concrete
imagery to express more abstract or psychological thoughts or feelings

that otherwise would remain lifeless, vague, purely mental. Thoreau, as in the two passages already quoted, prefers the word "trope" to metaphor and simile, at least partly because of its etymology aligning it with "turn," as he uses it in the following: "As in the expression of moral truths we admire any closeness to the physical fact which in all languages is the symbol of the spiritual, so finally, when natural objects are described, it is an advantage if words derived originally from nature, it is true, but which have been turned (*tropes*) from their primary signification to a moral sense are used" (*Journal*, XIII:145). The process can and should go in both directions. The language maker finds or tries to find in spiritual words their natural meaning and uses natural words in more than just their natural senses. Purely primitive language by itself would not be poetic, because it would be literal and univocal, with no higher dimension. Moreover, in using the tension implied in "troping," or turning, Thoreau emphasizes the frequent distance, or "stretch," between the natural and the spiritual, as well as the correspondences and similarities, for without this stretch the metaphors would carry no interest or surprise.

Thoreau, then, will often use puns—particularly puns that are etymological or pseudoetymological—not to embellish his prose or merely make his points with more wit but as a central way of relating to the world, infusing the natural with meaning and the abstract with body. The mental and the physical are united—or reunited—through the additional yoking of sound as well as sense. To keep our own discussion from becoming too abstract, we will look immediately at further examples. "In any weather, at any hour of the day or night, I have been anxious to improve the nick of time, and notch it on my stick too" (17). As we read the first clause, "the nick of time," we take it as the worn expression it is, almost a single compound word. But as we read "notch it on my stick too," we have to reconsider the phrase in terms of its component words, both because of a restored physical context and because of its syntax—the pronoun "it" makes us subliminally return to the earlier clause to identify its referent. Further, the alliteration between "nick" and "notch" and the repeated "t," "i," and "ck" sounds increase our awareness of the words as individual sounds. The rest of the sentence restores the physical image of "nick" as a small line: "to stand on the meeting of two eternities, the past and the future, which is precisely the present moment; to toe that line." Just as the mention of "line" helps us visualize "nick," the entire context helps us resee the expression "toe the line." I have had students write in their own papers, "tow the line," a mistake they would never have made had they read this sentence. Most of the ways we have of conceiving time rely on spatial metaphors—even nonverbal metaphors, like an hourglass or a clock face. This sentence renews our sense of time as space, giving a physical actuality to such temporal concepts as past, present, future, and eternity.

There are other occasions when Thoreau refurbishes a temporal cliché, as when he exclaims, "As if you could kill time without injuring eternity" (8), wherein a certain literalness is restored to "kill" through the use of "injuring." Later, Thoreau talks about having owned a boat that "after passing from hand to hand, has gone down the stream of time" (85). All of this prepares us for the famous paragraph beginning: "Time is but the stream I go a-fishing in. I drink at it. . . . Its thin current slides away" (98). The incrustations around "the stream of time" begin to get chipped off as one boats, fishes in it, and drinks from it. The pun on "current" as both "now"—"The present was my next experiment of this kind" (84)—and as the movement of that stream enhances the effect.

Often this revitalizing of worn expressions carries over from sentence to sentence, from paragraph to paragraph, creating networks of refreshening. On the third page, for example, Thoreau says of his self-oppressed townspeople, "Better if they had been born in the open pasture and suckled by a wolf, that they might have seen with clearer eyes what field they were called to labor in" (5), where "open pasture" restores physicality to "field," which otherwise might mean just a discipline or profession. The next-to-last sentence repeats the word "labor" but focuses us on the word "cultivate": "The portionless, who struggle with no such unnecessary inherited encumbrances, find it labor enough to subdue and cultivate a few cubic feet of flesh" (5). The beginning of the next paragraph, though, does pivot on "labor":

"But men labor under a mistake" (5), meaning the particular mistake they labor under is that they have to labor as hard as they do.

Repeatedly in *Walden*, Thoreau is able to polish the tarnished lamps of our language, our most tired sayings, to release a trapped but powerful genie. Even when he wishes to mock a kind of language, he cannot help but restore its physicality, as when he spoofs the conventions of contemporary romances: "Neither did the course of their true love run smooth—at any rate, how it did run and stumble, and get up again and go on!" (105). Leaning on the same word later, he writes, "A man sits as many risks as he runs" (153). When his tailoress tells him he cannot have a certain style because "They do not make them so now," he thinks about it, "emphasizing to myself each word separately that I may come at the meaning of it" (25). It seems as if he listens to all language like this, word by word, attending to each as if it were italicized.

While these examples often focus on multiple meanings of individual words, what they deconstruct and reconstruct are phrases or sayings that have themselves become almost conglomerate words. Just as often, Thoreau will train his reanimating energy on individual words, as in, "Let us rise early and fast, or break fast" (97). One has to read on tiptoe to catch many of these, as when he talks about the emphasis on luxury rather than safety in railroad cars, loaded with "ottomans, and sunshades, and a hundred other oriental things, which we are taking west with us" (37). The relative clause reminds us of the root of "oriental" in rising from the East, suggesting how we Americans are perpetuating this love of luxury by moving it west with us as we go, just as we are reminded of the geographic origins of "ottomans." Writing elsewhere of trains, Thoreau notes, "With such huge and lumbering civility the country hands a chair to the city" (115–16). "Lumbering civility" is an oxymoron, with the two puns playing off each other; the adjective also suggests the material of chairs, and the noun comes from the Latin word for "city." In "The Pond in Winter" Thoreau describes the blocks of ice, once cut from the cover of the pond, melting back: "Thus the pond *recovered* the greater part" (296, emphasis added).

Languages

Sometimes, perhaps to save his readers and commentators trouble, Thoreau will even make explicit his etymological energies:

> Not long since I was present at the auction of a deacon's effects, for his life had not been ineffectual:—
> "The evil that men do lives after them."
> As usual, a great proportion was trumpery which had begun to accumulate in his father's day. Among the rest was a dried tapeworm. And now, after lying half a century in his garret and other dust holes, these things were not burned; instead of a *bonfire*, or purifying destruction of them, there was an *auction*, or increasing of them. The neighbors eagerly collected to view them, bought them all, and carefully transported them to their garrets and dust holes, to lie there till their estates are settled, when they will start again. When a man dies he kicks the dust.
>
> (67–68)

"Bonfire," broken up into its components of bon + fire is seen as a good or beneficent fire that cleanses; "auction" is seen as sharing the same root as "augment," an increasing here not only of owners but of dust. Other etymologies are made almost explicit, as the turning of "ineffectual" to mean "without effects," which is accomplished by using "effects" five words earlier. Others we must be aware of ourselves—such as "settled," meaning both "disposed of" and, more physically, "remaining still" so that the dust can reaccumulate on them. Even the line from Shakespeare is not simply quoted for adornment or authority but is reread in a more physical context, the "evil" here being all the glorified junk we accumulate, bought with the money that is the even deeper root of it all. These techniques culminate what could be called a conflation of two euphemisms for dying, both of which had become so worn as to conjure up nothing physical—biting the dust and kicking the bucket. Thoreau shuffles these to redefine death after a conventional, "effectual" life as stirring up the dust from all one's possessions.

Much of Thoreau's wordplay like that just presented has struck readers as clowning with the pun, the lowest form of humor, especially when one doesn't think of it first. But in Thoreau's hands the pun is mightier than just the word, for it becomes a special case of metaphor. That is, things are linked to each other not only through sense but through similar, sometimes identical sound. And it is really the trope, not the sometimes etymological, sometimes merely fortuitous coincidence of sound, that carries the brunt of the meaning. Here is a rather grim and elaborate example:

> If we do not get out sleepers, and forge rails, and devote days and nights to the work, but go to tinkering upon our *lives* to improve *them*, who will build railroads? . . . We do not ride on the railroad; it rides upon us. Did you ever think what those sleepers are that underlie the railroad? Each one is a man, an Irish-man or a Yankee man. The rails are laid on them, and they are covered with sand, and the cars run smoothly over them. They are sound sleepers I assure you. And every few years a new lot is laid down and run over; so that, if some have the pleasure of riding on a rail, others have the misfortune to be ridden upon. And when they run over a man that is walking in his sleep, a supernumerary sleeper in the wrong position, and wake him up, they suddenly stop the cars, and make a hue and cry about it, as if this were an exception. I am glad to know that it takes a gang of men for every five miles to keep the sleepers down and level in their beds as it is, for this is a sign that they may sometime get up again.
>
> (92–93)

The notion of the railroad riding on us may seem just another version of Emerson's inversion, "Things are in the saddle, / And ride mankind." But the link between "sleepers" as rail supports and "sleepers" as human is a pun elaborated with such metaphoric intensity that it turns general social concern into an immediate human empathy; riding on a railroad becomes as unpleasant as being ridden on a rail. What begins as a phonetic similarity within a single word is woven into one of the basic oppositions in the book, that between sleep and waking. Further, the drawing out of this pun activates the dormant puns in other words in this passage, such as "beds" and "sign." The pun/metaphor is detailed and powerful enough for Thoreau to count on us remembering it 150 pages later, when he talks about the once "boundless chestnut woods of Lincoln,—they now sleep their long sleep under the railroad" (238).

Puns like these are not flourishes of style or a witty dress to an already-conceived message, but central to the book's strategies. But how far or how extensively can this way of refurbishing language go? What are its possibilities and its limits? To probe this idea further, we can look at one more extended example, beginning with its prototype in Emerson's *Nature*:

> When we speak of nature in this manner, we have a distinct but most poetical sense in the mind. We mean the integrity of impression made by manifold natural objects. It is this which distinguishes the stick of timber of the wood-cutter, from the tree of the poet. The charming landscape which I saw this morning, is indubitably made up of some twenty or thirty farms. Miller owns this field, Locke that, and Manning the woodland beyond. But none of them owns the landscape. There is a property in the horizon which no man has but he whose eyes can integrate all the parts, that is, the poet. This is the best part of these men's farms, yet to this their warranty-deeds give no title.
>
> —Emerson, 9

This passage helps to concretize a related series of distinctions that Emerson makes at more philosophical length in *Nature* and elsewhere—between the rational, analytic "understanding" and the more intuitive "Reason," between that which dissects and divides and that which apprehends holistically. The related images of the stick of timber as opposed to the tree, and of the carving up of the earth into rectangles of plots as opposed to the horizon make these distinctions more graspable, but the muted wordplay helps. Though Locke was indeed a real Concord farmer, the use of his name here also suggests a rational-istically limited epistemology. The use of "integrity" along with "inte-grate" suggests the ability to see wholeness or oneness. Ironically, the best "part" of each farm is its contribution to this "whole." "Property" is transferred from its meaning to the "understanding" to a more philosophical quality or essence apparent to the Reason. The deeds give no "title," both in the sense that they cannot provide "ownership" since by definition to own is to lose, and in the sense that they cannot even name or give a title to this "property"—only poetry or polyphonous prose like this can.

Although the word "poet" does not appear in Thoreau's version, the passage was published separately in *Sartain's Union Magazine* in 1852 under the title "A Poet Buying a Farm":

> At a certain season of our life we are accustomed to consider every spot as the possible site of a house. I have thus surveyed the country on every side within a dozen miles of where I live. In imagination I have bought all the farms in succession, for all were to be bought, and I knew their price. I walked over each farmer's premises, tasted his wild apples, discoursed on husbandry with him, took his farm at his price, at any price, mortgaging it to him in my mind; even put a higher price on it,—took every thing but a deed of it,—took his word for his deed, for I dearly love to talk,—cultivated it, and him too to some extent, I trust, and withdrew when I had enjoyed it long enough, leaving him to carry it on. This experience entitled me to be regarded as a sort of real-estate broker by my friends. Wherever I sat, there I might live, and the landscape radiated from me accordingly.
>
> (81)

As in the passage from Emerson, the punning is not random or haphazard; instead, each double entendre splits into two separate levels of perception and meaning: (a) that of the understanding, the "common-sense" level of business and ownership—and we remember that Thoreau noted that "the commonest sense is the sense of men asleep" (325)—and (b) the more poetic level of the Reason. On the first level, "site" is a place to build; on the second, it is "sight," a place to be seen and to see from—just as "survey" means both to lay out into lots, like Locke's and Manning's, and to scan, to behold. Thoreau has "bought all the farms in succession," at first seemingly getting the right of ownership to pass to him next but really possessing them in perception one right after the next to form a landscape or horizon. The "premises" he walks over are first the land itself, next the clause of ownership in the deed, and then the farmer's very ideas or assumptions about the world. While this pun moves toward the abstract, "deed" moves toward the concrete, from a legal document to an actual action, just as "his word," his promise, moves to his very conversation, the word he utters. And talk is not cheap here but, rather, "dear" in both senses. The zeugma "cultivating it and him too" turns this yoke into a joke on planting a field and making one's conversation partner more cultured—as we have seen, one of Thoreau's favorite puns. The entire experience gives him the "title" of "real-estate broker," seeing beyond the false estates established by deeds and surveys to break us into our real estate, which is all creation. The sheer virtuosity of this verbal performance is impressive. Thoreau said, "In writing, conversation should be folded many times thick."[3] Here the verbal texture becomes so thick as to be almost opaque, and we are not really given the verbal and imaginative possession of the farm it argues for. There is the danger that the farm here will also become a parable of a farm, that we will get so far into the labyrinth of language that we will lose our threads of connection and return. Can we more actively fashion a new language that is not built on the ruins of an old one? The challenge is particularly immediate to American writers, who find themselves working in a language named for another country—English. Thoreau expressed the dilemma thus:

> Natural objects and phenomena are the original symbols or types which express our thoughts and feelings, yet American scholars, having little or no root in the soil, commonly strive with all their might to confine themselves to the imported symbols alone. All the true growth and experience, the living speech, they would fain reject as "Americanisms." It is the old error, which the church, the state, the school ever commit, choosing darkness rather than light, holding fast to the old and to tradition. A more intimate knowledge, a deeper experience, will surely originate a word. When I really know that our river pursues a serpentine course of the Merrimack, shall I continue to describe it by referring to some other river no older than itself which is like it, and call it a *meander*? It is no more *meandering* than the Meander is *musketaquidding*. As well sing of the nightingale here as the Meander. What if there were a tariff on words, on language, for the encouragement of home manufactures? Have we not genius to distinguish the true from the counterfeit?
>
> —*Journal*, XII:389–90

If one, though, were to use the word "musketaquidding," would others understand? Instead of coining new individual words, Thoreau often uses a slew of old ones to describe something with specificity and precision: "I have discerned a matchless and indescribable light blue, such as watered or changeable silks and sword blades suggest, more cerulean than the sky itself, alternating with the original dark green on the opposite sides of the waves, which last appeared but muddy in comparison. It is a vitreous greenish blue, as I remember it, like those patches of the winter sky seen through cloud vistas in the west before sundown" (177). We know that Walden is both green and blue, since "lying between the earth and the heavens, it partakes of the color of both" (176). But this passage is less a meditation on its symbolic intermediary value than an attempt to describe an exact color that is "indescribable" only in that no one word exists to describe it. This tendency to describe experience exactly could use a great many words; imagine the results had Thoreau taken such care and imagination to describe every shade in his surroundings.

While this strategy tends to multiply words and make them more precise, Thoreau often employs with it a counterstrategy, which is to draw on all the resources of language, not just meaning but rhythm and texture, making the language both more compressed and more suggestive. To some extent, all accomplished writers do the same thing; Thoreau, however, often does so in a particularly intense and self-conscious way, deliberately trying to fashion his own more physical language. Every word not only means something—it is something, something that as readers we first apprehend as black marks on paper but that mentally, at least, we turn back into sound, air pushed up from the lungs through throats, tongue, and teeth. As we have seen in chapter 5, Thoreau regards this joining of the past—the already formed—with the present—the living voice, one of the most enticing potentials of literature as a medium: "A written word . . . is the work of art nearest to life itself. It may be translated into every language, and not only be read but actually breathed from all human lips;—not be represented on canvas or in marble only, but be carved out of the breath of life itself" (102). At another point he says we would do better to listen to the whistle of the engine or the ringing of a bell not as signals to run toward or from but as sounds in themselves—"We will consider what kind of music they are like" (97)—a mental shift we should apply to words in a literary work as well.

To analyze this music in detail, to talk directly about what might be most effective subliminally, is to risk letting some of the magic evaporate, just as I may have muted some of Thoreau's humor by explaining several of his puns. Yet my hope is that this very process will make the reader more sensitive to all the hundreds of other examples appearing throughout the book. The first passage whose sounds I want to emphasize is from "Solitude," although it might just as appropriately fit in the preceding chapter, "Sounds":

> This is a delicious evening, when the whole body is one sense, and imbibes delight through every pore. I go and come with a strange liberty in Nature, a part of herself. As I walk along the stony shore of the pond in my shirt sleeves, though it is cool as well as cloudy and windy, and I see nothing special to attract me, all the elements are unusually congenial to me. The bullfrogs trump to usher in the night, and the note of the whippoorwill is borne on the rippling wind from over the water. Sympathy with the fluttering alder and poplar leaves almost takes away my breath; yet, like the lake, my serenity is rippled but not ruffled. These small waves raised by the evening wind are as remote from storm as the smooth reflecting surface. Though it is now dark, the wind still blows and roars in the wood, the waves still dash, and some creatures lull the rest with their notes.
>
> (129)

The first two words help alert us to the sound play here, as the second is part of the first, creating an echoing or rippling effect: "Th*is is*." These words, together with "delicious," prepare the reader for the "s" and "sh" sounds that run through the passage. One way Thoreau improves on Emerson's language is to triangulate the senses—we usually apply "delicious" more to an apple than to an evening, but together with "imbibe" the word suggests a taking in of the world, making it part of ourselves and vice versa. Objects that are only seen are experienced as external to self, but those tasted and drunk, especially through every pore, are more intimate, touching bodies more directly. That Thoreau is even more concerned than usual with the sounds of words is evinced in the phrase "like the lake." Most of the time, of course, Walden is a "pond"; here, however, the phrase extends the kinds of echoes or sound reflections that we see in combinations like "alder and poplar," "shore . . . shirt," "rippled . . . ruffled," and "cool . . . cloudy." Just as the speaker increasingly feels himself a part of nature, the sounds of the words increasingly relate to what they describe. In this sentence, for example, the short "u" sounds predominate in talking about the frogs; then the more trilling "w" and "l" sounds take over: "The bullfrogs trump to usher in the night, and the note of the whippoorwill is borne on the rippling wind from over the water." Both the frogs and the whippoorwills were important for their sounds in the preceding chapter of that name, as they are here, at the beginning of this one as well. A "whippoorwill" itself is named for the sound it makes, and the introduction of this bird signals the increasingly onomatopoeic texture as darkness falls in the passage and the sense of hearing necessarily becomes predominant: "Though it is now dark, the wind still blows and roars in the wood, the waves still dash and some creatures lull the rest with their notes." "Dash" and "roars" are the two most obvious onomatopoeic words, but that quality spills into the rhythms and sound interweavings of the entire sentence, especially with the "s" and "sh" sounds suggesting the regular lapping on the shore of the waves.

Because writing is a medium of sounds, Thoreau can effect a more direct mimesis than he could with other senses, as in the phrase "the music of a thousand tinkling rills and rivulets" (304). Still, as F. O. Matthiessen first discussed, Thoreau is also capable of writing a vividly kinesthetic prose that appropriates the rhythms of the actions being presented. Here are two examples Matthiessen missed: "At length you slowly raise, pulling hand over hand, some horned pout squeaking and squirming to the upper air" (175). The clustered accented monosyllables, the repeated "o" sounds, the repetitions ("hand over hand," "*squeaking* and *squirming*")—all help to render the order and pace of the experience. Sometimes the word placement and rhythm parallel not so much the physical action as the trajectory of the emotion itself: "Ah! I have penetrated to those meadows on the morning of many a first spring day, jumping from hummock to hummock, from willow root to willow root, when the wild river valley and the woods were bathed in so pure and bright a light as would have waked the dead, if they had been slumbering in their graves, as some suppose" (317). The accented "Ah" modulating into "I" is powerful.

> *Jum*ping from h*um*mock
> to h*um*mock
> from willow root
> to willow root

captures the action well, but even more it mirrors—as does the syntax of the entire sentence—the exuberance that, as soon as one expects it to end, picks up more energy for yet another subordinate clause or two.

So far we have seen two of Thoreau's strategies for making language lively: (a) his restoring or reinventing the physicality that has become too implicit and (b) his fashioning of new languages. A third strategy—one harder to discuss, because it resides less in specific sentences and paragraphs than in the spaces between them—is Thoreau's range as a stylist, his juxtaposing not only different but often opposing styles. Other American writers considered stylists, such as Henry James, William Faulkner, and Ernest Hemingway, write prose with a certain unmistakable personal signature. Their sentences could not be confused with one another's, or with anybody else's, at a distance of 30 paces. Thoreau, by contrast, has no characteristic sentence length or construction, no single register. The writer perhaps most like him is Herman Melville, in that the prose of both is marked more by its range and versatility, its dizzying leaps from the scientific to the sublime and from the colloquial to the rhapsodic, than by a single sustained voice.

Thoreau, for example, reduces some of his Walden experience beyond even sentences to give us tables, such as the one on page 59, which itemizes what he ate and the expense of each item to the half-cent. Yet a few pages later he minimizes and even jettisons that level of literal account: "There is a certain class of unbelievers who sometimes ask me such questions as, if I think that I can live on vegetable food alone; and to strike at the root of the matter at once,—for the root is faith,—I am accustomed to answer such, that I can live on board nails. If they cannot understand that, they cannot understand much that I have to say" (64–65). This notion might help explain why the sum for nails is so disproportionately high in another table (49), which was an anomaly until Roland Robbins excavated the cabin site in 1945 and found hundreds of bent nails.

We can note similar variations on virtually any page of *Walden*. Here, to take another example at random, are two adjoining paragraphs from "The Bean-Field":

> This is the result of my experience in raising beans. Plant the common small white bush bean about the first of June, in rows three feet by eighteen inches apart, being careful to select fresh round and unmixed seed. First look out for worms, and supply vacancies by planting anew. Then look out for woodchucks, if it is an exposed place, for they will nibble off the earliest tender leaves almost clean as they go; and again, when the young tendrils make their appearance, they have notice of it, and will shear them off with both buds and young pods, sitting erect like a squirrel. But above all harvest as early as possible, if you would escape frosts and have a fair and saleable crop; you may save much loss by this means.
>
> (163)

This passage leaves a commentator with about as much to do as Maytag would have us believe about its repairman. It means so exactly what it says that any summary or paraphrase would be redundant or distorting.

The next paragraph is different enough that Thoreau uses an entire and redundant sentence for the transition—"This *further* experience *also* I gained" (163, emphasis added):

> I said to myself, I will not plant beans and corn with so much industry another summer, but such seeds, if the seed is not lost, as

sincerity, truth, simplicity, faith, innocence, and the like, and see if they will not grow in this soil, even with less toil and manurance, and sustain me, for surely it has not been exhausted for these crops. Alas! I said this to myself; but now another summer is gone, and another, and another, and I am obliged to say to you, Reader, that the seeds which I planted, if indeed they *were* the seeds of those virtues, were wormeaten or had lost their vitality, and so did not come up.

(163–64)

As opposed to the direct address in the first paragraph—the implied subject in each of the sentences after the first is "you"—here we are told twice that Thoreau is talking to himself, turning our relationship into that of eavesdropper to an internal monologue. The syntax accordingly turns on itself; instead of straightforward directives, we get longer sentences with more subordinate clauses, more ifs, ands, and buts. The paragraph is more allusive, more interconnected with other parts of the chapter and with other texts, such as the Bible.

An oversimplified reading of the two paragraphs could suggest that the first centers on the natural fact, the second on the spiritual fact, thus fulfilling Thoreau's stated intention of raising beans primarily to serve a parable maker. Yet such a reading implies a certain hierarchy of value that, if anything, *Walden* hopes to invert. An antiparabolic parable from the "Conclusion" is relevant here: "In sane moments we regard only the facts, the case that is. Say what you have to say, not what you ought. Any truth is better than make-believe. Tom Hyde, the tinker, standing on the gallows, was asked if he had any thing to say. 'Tell the tailors,' said he, 'to remember to make a knot in their thread before they take the first stitch.' His companion's prayer is forgotten" (327–28). Like the companion's justly forgotten prayer, the second paragraph is more subjective and subjunctive, appealing imploringly to some higher world of spirit or abstraction. The first tells us how to raise beans.

The stylistic variation throughout the book is more than just an attempt to add something like "variety" to the reading experience; instead, it carries with it a stance toward reality that is treated in more detail in chapter 8 of this volume. We can approach this stance through a passage—from *A Week*—on the limitations of even Jesus's exemplary life: "Yet he taught mankind but imperfectly how to live; his thoughts were all directed toward another world. There is another kind of success than his. Even here we have a sort of living to get, and must buffet it somewhat longer. There are various tough problems yet to solve, and we must make shift to live, betwixt spirit and matter, such a human life as we can" (*A Week*, 74). The shifting styles of the book indicate the experience of being buffeted between opposing realms: of matter and spirit, of the literal and the figurative, of outer and inner. If the variety of languages suggests any one viewpoint, it is that "The universe is wider than our views of it" (320). Reality is fluid, changing, and ultimately mysterious, and no one language or formulation can capture that much of it. The most one can hope to do is triangulate it from a number of vantages.

One verbal strategy we can fasten on as evincing this approach to reality is what we may call the self-revising sentence—a sentence that rethinks, qualifies, or even contradicts itself before our eyes, as in the very first words in the book: "When I wrote the following pages, or rather the bulk of them. . . ." (3). Surely in the years of composition Thoreau had the time to revise this into something like "When I wrote most of the following pages . . ."; nevertheless, the sentence as it appears conveys not just its information but the sense of mind reaching for exactness at the same time it recognizes its elusiveness.

In "Reading" we are told that "Books must be read as deliberately and reservedly as they were written" (101). The root of "deliberately" is "to weigh," and Thoreau often presents his own sentences with this deliberate weighing of each word foregrounded, as in the following:

What a man thinks of himself, that it is which determines, or rather indicates, his fate.

(7)

I have thoroughly tried school-keeping, and found that my expenses were in proportion, or rather out of proportion, to my income.

(60)

He was so simply and naturally humble—if he can be called humble who never aspires.

(147)

He told me, with the utmost simplicity and truth, quite superior, or rather *inferior*, to any thing that is called humility, that he was "deficient in intellect."

(151)

There have been many stories told about the bottom, or rather no bottom, of this pond, which certainly had no foundation for themselves.

(285)

My favorite appears on the page before the last example, in describing the color of Walden's pickerel: "They are not green like the pines, nor gray like the stones, nor blue like the sky; but they have, to my eyes, if possible, yet rarer colors" (284). The "if possible" cues us that Thoreau has remembered in midsentence what he seems to have forgotten in beginning to write it, that the color of pines, stones, and sky are themselves rare and miraculous. As Emily Dickinson writes, "To hear an Oriole sing / May be a common thing—/ Or only a divine."[4] Both this deliberate rephrasing and the more general strategy of keeping the prose cross-grained and roughly textured, then, are attempts to involve the reader more directly not only in the experiences related but in the processes and problematics of the writing itself.

Emerson saw the poets as liberating gods, not because of any specific content but because they use their fresher language to spring us out of the prison house of conventional language. Though all language is metaphorical, sometimes we let those metaphors harden, and mistake the structure of our language for the structure of reality. This Emersonian vision challenged the literary artist to move from the fringes of American society to its epistemological center, a challenge Thoreau took up, waking his neighbors up to the ways they make speech. The languages of *Walden* are the best evidence of the success of the pondside experiment.

7

Paradise (To Be) Regained
The Visionary Gleam

In Concord's Sleepy Hollow Cemetery Thoreau's grave is marked with a stone that reads simply "Henry," in an unassuming plot that also covers his parents and his three siblings. The family line ends here, since, like their famous brother, Helen, John, and Sophia Thoreau had no children of their own. But a few steps from this family plot is buried a spiritual heir, a woman in whose childhood Henry was a vital and formative presence, Ellen Tucker Emerson, first child of Lydian and Ralph Waldo. The epitaph on her more imposing gravestone is as follows:

> Her life was happy in that
> "Among the scenes of real life, she wrought
> Upon the plan that pleased her childish thought."

I have been unable to track down the author of the couplet in the quotation marks—I like to think it was Ellen herself—but the spirit behind them is that of Henry D. Thoreau. The lines suggest that Ellen Emerson was able to embody in her own life a central aspect of his vision, a vision he makes explicit in a letter she received when she was

10: "I suppose you think that persons who are as old as your father and myself are always thinking about very grave things, but I know that we are meditating the same old themes that we did when we were ten years old, only we go more gravely about it. You love to write or to read a fairy story and that is what you will always like to do, in some form or other. By and by you will discover that you want what are called the necessaries of life only that you may realize some such dream" (*Correspondence*, 245). I find the passage, especially its last sentence, something of a key to *Walden*; it helps us see more of the purpose and the point, for example, to the long first section on how to best get the "necessaries of life." In inverting our customary goals, in putting the reality principle in the service of the pleasure principle, the passage glosses sentences like "If men would steadily observe realities only, and not allow themselves to be deluded, life, to compare it with such things as we know, would be like a fairy tale and the Arabian Nights' Entertainments" (95) and "Children, who play life, discern its true law and relations more clearly than men, who fail to live it worthily" (96).

The most important word in the letter is "realize," meaning not only its usual sense of understanding or recognizing but its more etymological one of "making real." It is the same double sense with which Thoreau uses the word in the last paragraph of *Walden*—"I do not say that John or Jonathan will realize all this" (333) or in describing the coming in of spring as "the realization of the Golden Age" (313). And it is in this sense that all of *Walden* can be said to be a story of realization, of turning childhood thoughts, dreams, and ideals into deeds in the world and into physical presences like huts, beanfields, and books, for it is also significant in this letter that "to write" a fairy tale is emphasized even more than to read one, through a reversal of the usual word order. One is not so much to engage in passive reveries as to actively turn those reveries into something tangible outside the mind. One of the most famous passages in *Walden* epitomizes not only its subject matter but its own coming into being: "If you have built castles in the air, your work need not be lost; that is where they should be. Now put the foundations under them" (324). It is this quotation that another Emerson child, Edward, in his warm reminiscences, chose as best epitomizing Thoreau's "religion."[1]

This chapter traces that impulse to "realize" one's childhood, both in Thoreau's work as a whole and, more extensively, in *Walden*. In the latter what initially might be personal longings are turned into more widely applicable cultural symbols; the psychological becomes increasingly mythological. These mythological terms, especially those of the paradise stories of Eden and the Golden Age and their analogues in the pastoral, are then used as counters to depict a consciousness that can best be termed "visionary," a kind of holistic being in the world that combines infant joys with mature religious aspirations. These moments of visionary intensity occur throughout *Walden*, as glimpses of fulfillments of goals toward which much of the book is vectored.

Of course, this very reverence for childhood was partly a cultural construct for Thoreau, who, along with other transcendentalists like Bronson Alcott and Elizabeth Peabody, embraced this romantic idealization, most famously expressed in Wordsworth's ode "Intimations of Immortality from Recollections of Early Childhood":

> Heaven lies about us in our infancy!
> Shades of the prison-house begin to close
> Upon the growing Boy,
> But He beholds the light, and whence it flows,
> He sees it in his joy;
> The Youth, who daily farther from the East
> Must travel, still is Nature's Priest,
> And by the vision splendid
> Is on his way attended;
> At length the Man perceives it die away,
> And fade into the light of common day.[2]

In Thoreau's journals we see these conventions, including paraphrase and misquotation from the ode, put in the service of what must also be a deeply felt personal vision:

Paradise (To Be) Regained

Methinks my present experience is nothing my past experience is all in all. I think that no experience which I have to-day comes up to or is comparable with the experiences of my boyhood-And not only this is true-but as far back as I can remember I have unconsciously referred to the experiences of a previous state of existence. "Our life is a forgetting" &c

Formerly methought nature developed as I developed and grew up with me. My life was extacy. In youth before I lost any of my senses, I can remember that I was all alive—and inhabited my body with inexpressible satisfaction, both its weariness & its refreshment were sweet to me. This earth was the most glorious musical instrument, and I was audience to its strains. To have such sweet impressions made on us—such extacies begotten of the breezes. I can remember how I was astonished. I said to myself-I said to others-There comes into my mind or soul an indescribable infinite all absorbing divine heavenly pleasure, a sense of elevation & expansion—and have had nought to do with it. I perceive that I am dealt with by superior powers. This is a pleasure, a joy, an existence which I have not procured myself-I speak as a witness on the stand and tell what I have perceived The morning and the evening were sweet to me, and I lead a life aloof from society of men. . . . For years I marched as to a music in comparison with which the military music of the streets is noise & discord. I was daily intoxicated and yet no man could call me intemperate.

—*Journal*, 3:305–6

I quote at such length so that we can see some of the underlying emotional similarities and the artistic differences between these themes in the journals and in *Walden*. The tone, exuberant in its very losses, confirms another passage Thoreau wrote the year before: "My imagination, my love & reverence & admiration, my sense of the miraculous is not so excited by any event as by the remembrance of my youth" (*Journal*, 3:84). Rarely, even in the journals, does Thoreau talk about his own feelings and sensations unattached to a specific immediate object for so long and with such loose, excessive, and redundant rhetoric; the prose here is uncharacteristically archaic and literary: "Methinks," "methought," "begotten of the breezes." The list of adjectives following "indescribable" gives credence to that word, all of them overlapping yet none quite hitting the mark. The contrast between the sentence "For years I marched . . ." and its more famous *Walden* counterpart (326) shows the difference that small changes in diction and syntax can make. Similarly, the unremarkable "inexpressible satisfaction" becomes in *Walden* "a simple and irrepressible satisfaction with the gift of life" (78). Although this journal passage remains touching and describes that loss of exuberance with its own kind of energy, at times it approaches a kind of mawkishness, the kind that creeps into another comment on the Marlborough road: "There I can walk and recover the lost child that I am without any ringing of a bell" (*Journal*, 3:319). Often Thoreau in the journal seems to be writing the ode to dejection he abjures in the epigraph to *Walden*.

One of the achievements of *Walden* is that this nostalgia for the past is turned into a sense of prospectiveness, of potentiality. It is a book haunted by loss, but the possibilities for recovery are also pervasive. The references to childhood are submerged, subliminal, almost as out of reach as the experiences themselves have become, yet they lurk everywhere, lending some places and objects an elusive sanctification. After listing, for example, all the present attractions of the Hollowell farm, Thoreau admits that what draws him "above all" is "the recollection I had of it from my earliest voyages up the river" (83). One day Thoreau discovers the groundnut, "the potato of the aborigines, a sort of fabulous fruit, which I had begun to doubt if I had ever dug and eaten in childhood, as I had told, and had not dreamed it" (239). The text here, by the way, is probably corrupt: a "been" between "had" and "told" must have been dropped out unnoticed somewhere in the publishing process. In any case, that particular quality of uncertainty and interconnection between dream and actuality, between the fable and the life, emerges often in the book, as in the letter, when childhood memories are stirred.

Of all the places in the book, though, it is, of course, Walden Pond itself that receives the most resonance from this aura of childhood: "Though the woodchoppers have laid bare first this shore and then that, and the Irish have built their sties by it, and the railroad has infringed on its border, and the ice-men have skimmed it once, it is itself unchanged, the same water which my youthful eyes fell on; all the change is in me. It has not acquired one permanent wrinkle after all its ripples. It is perennially young and I may stand and see a swallow dip apparently to pick an insect from its surface as of yore" (192–93). This first long subordinate clause is a compendium of the various desecrations, described in detail in other parts of the book, that the shore has suffered since Thoreau's youth; a few pages later, out of a sense of honesty and complexity, he even adds himself to the violators: "Since the woodcutters, and the railroad, and I myself have profaned Walden . . ." (197). This admission, together with the contrast just cited between the unchanged pond and Thoreau's changed self would seem to stress the growing rift between the pond and him, between a nature of which he once felt himself an ecstatic part and his sole adult self. And yet that the pond itself still retains those qualities of freshness holds out the hope that these same qualities are still potentialities in Thoreau, still recoverable. Indeed, the very act of perceiving the life of the pond, as the last sentence in the passage suggests, goes a long way toward healing the rift between nature and the self, between the child and the man. That the swallow can perceive and capture a small insect on the large surface—and that Thoreau's eyes and pen are still keen enough to capture this moment—becomes an emblem of this hope. Another token of possibility is the fact that the shore restores itself through a pattern of cyclicity after the devastations: "Why, here is Walden, the same woodland lake that I discovered so many years ago; where a forest was cut down last winter another is springing up by its shore as lustily as ever; the same thought is welling up to its surface that was then; it is the same liquid joy and happiness to itself and its Maker, ay, and it *may* be to me" (193). The pun on "springing" both as an action and as a season carries over to "*may*," anticipating the relation between the natural seasons and human regeneration elaborated in the "Spring" chapter.

A passage near this one, both in the text and in its texture of feeling and image is the following;

> When I first paddled a boat on Walden, it was completely sur-
> rounded by thick and lofty pine and oak woods, and in some of its
> coves grape vines had run over the trees next the water and formed

bowers under which a boat could pass. The hills which form its shores are so steep, and the woods on them were then so high, that, as you looked down from the west end, it had the appearance of an amphitheatre for some kind of sylvan spectacle. I have spent many an hour, when I was younger, floating over its surface as the zephyr willed, having paddled my boat to the middle, and lying on my back across the seats, in a summer forenoon, dreaming awake, until I was aroused by the boat touching the sand, and I arose to see what shore my fates had impelled me to; days when idleness was the most attractive and productive industry. Many a forenoon have I stolen away, preferring to spend thus the most valued part of the day; for I was rich, if not in money, in sunny hours and summer days, and spent them lavishly; nor do I regret that I did not waste more of them in the workshop or the teacher's desk.

(191–92)

The sentences here are long, lazy, lingering. As in the groundnut passage, there is a quality of "dreaming awake," of combining clear, vivid physical images with an oneiric sense of psychological power and appropriateness. The landscape is objectively actual while at the same time creating a sense of a large, nurturing nature embracing—embowering—its human child. The thick forest imagery invokes Milton's descriptions of paradise, except here the mount becomes an enclosure, just as in the Indian "fable" (182) a hill is turned inside out to form the pond. Although Thoreau knows something is bogus about this story, he mentions it, it seems, "to link his facts to fable," just as he does "a faint recollection of a little fish some five inches long" (184). There is the sense of complete abandonment to nature, with the secure knowledge that nowhere its winds blow him would be dangerous or malevolent; Thoreau can lie down at his ease, cradled by the boat, the pond, and the surrounding hills, engaged in a revery that is at once fully conscious and pleasantly lulling. The pun that is almost subliminal in the initial "spent" becomes explicit in its second context, as Thoreau further contrasts this state of pure being with the goal-directed, economic motives of his neighbors. The boyhood experiences blend imperceptibly with his adult experiences at the pond, now at the time of writing also in the past, for we are unsure about when he was rich in sunny hours: in this recaptured childhood or in his later life, when working in the shop or classroom was indeed a real alternative.

The passage that best evokes Thoreau's childhood feelings in relation to his later dwelling by the pond, the passage in which the external world most effectively becomes a landscape of the mind without losing its own actuality, is the second paragraph of "The Bean-Field":

> When I was four years old, as I well remember, I was brought from Boston to this my native town, through these very woods and this field, to the pond. It is one of the oldest scenes stamped on my memory. And now to-night my flute has waked the echoes over that very water. The pines still stand here older than I; or, if some have fallen, I have cooked my supper with their stumps, and a new growth is rising all around, preparing another aspect for new infant eyes. Almost the same johnswort springs from the same perennial root in this pasture, and even I have at length helped to clothe that fabulous landscape of my infant dreams, and one of the results of my presence and influence is seen in these bean leaves, corn blades, and potato vines.
>
> (155–56)

Although the language of the first sentence is clear and simple, we are a little disoriented as to place here, as we just were with time, somewhat as in a dream. How can a youthful excursion from home be to Thoreau's "native" town? We can begin to get our bearings when we learn the biographical facts. Thoreau was indeed born in Concord, without seeing or remembering the pond. The next year, though, the family moved first to Chelmsford and then to Boston, returning to Concord permanently the following year.

But more than this biographical information, what makes sense of this passage is the logic of myth and psychology. During the composition of *Walden* Thoreau wrote in his journal, "Facts should only be as the frame to my pictures; they should be material to the mythology which I am writing. . . . I would so state facts that they shall be myths or mythologic" (*Journal*, III:99). On this level the trip to Walden represents a journey back to the sources of one's being. It is a voyage from the circumference—represented by an exile in a city, Boston, now the eastern terminus to the railroad that now skirts the pond—through woods and the field, to the center itself, the pond. This visit at the age of 4 (actually, Thoreau was 5, as he remembers more accurately in his journal) is also a prefiguration of his move at 28 to reside here. Indeed, three days after he made this later journey, he described it in richly mythological terms: "I am glad to remember tonight as I sit by my door that I too am at least a remote descendent of that heroic race of men of whom there is a tradition. I too sit here on the shore of my Ithaca, a fellow wanderer and survivor of Ulysses" (*Journal*, 2:156). After a period of forced exile, the hero completes his journey to a scene of homecoming and recognition. Thus, Thoreau links the fact of his life to fable, realizes a fairy tale in the conditions of his being.

The passage, then, conjures up the past, but primarily to intensify the immediate in place and in time, as emphasized in the first sentence: "*this* my native town," "*these very* woods and *this* field." The next sentence shifts the verb tense into the present, where it will remain for the rest of the paragraph, and the following sentence reinforces this immediacy by beginning "And *now to-night*." The passage is about repetition in that Thoreau's current residence reflects a childhood experience that in some ways repeats or returns even earlier primal experiences beyond the reach of memory and articulation. And this repetition is enacted by recurring sounds, "echoes," to use the terms of the passage itself. The first sentence particularly is an intricate pattern of repetition: "When I was . . . as I well . . . I was," "*br ough t* from B o st on," "to . . . through . . . to," "this . . . these . . . this." And throughout the passage, words and phrases echo each other: "very woods . . . very water," "new growth . . . new infant eyes," "almost the same . . . the same." The last pairing is especially significant, because it reminds us that a repetition, even if exact, is not simply a duplication; it is different at the least in coming later. As Thoreau says elsewhere in *Walden*, "[T]he echo is, to some extent, an original sound" (123), for important differences are registered within the very echoes, as we hear, if we read on tiptoe, "John's word," the sounds of his irrevocably lost brother in "johnswort," which is just "almost the same."

Paradise (To Be) Regained

The crucial change—and what makes the present experience original—is registered in the words "even I have at length helped to clothe that fabulous landscape of my infant dreams." Thoreau has clothed it in two ways: (a) he has planted it with his own crops, the main activity of this chapter, and (b) he has put it into the words we are reading. He has decided what kinds of plants shall grow and how, and he has circumscribed the landscape with what he calls elsewhere "the most admirable kind of invisible fence" (83), giving a kind of permanence to the inevitably transitory dreams of youth. In this paragraph Thoreau has infused his personal life history with the resonance of myth, so much so that he does what Emerson says the poet should do: "write his autobiography in colossal cipher, or into universality" (Emerson, 465).

We can see aspects of this universalizing process and can catch some of the resonances that have become muted in the *Walden* passage by looking also at the journal entry on which it is based: "Twenty three years since when I was 5 years old, I was brought from Boston to this pond, away in the country which was then but another name for the extended world for me—one of the most ancient scenes stamped on the tablets of my memory—the oriental asiatic valley of my world— whence so many races and inventions have gone forth in recent times. That woodland vision for a long time made the drapery of my dreams" (*Journal*, 2:173–74). In this entry Thoreau's childhood is explicitly linked with the childhood of the human race, for it was believed in nineteenth-century America that the Garden of Eden was in an Asiatic valley. Thoreau's journey back to his native town, then, is a microcosmic version of the race going so far forth from this paradise that eventually it circles back to it. This was to be Walt Whitman's theme in poems like "Facing West from California's Shores" and "Passage to India," but as early as in *A Week* Thoreau has encompassed it in a single sentence, punning again on "orientalism": "As we have said, there is an orientalism in the most restless pioneer, and the farthest west is but the farthest east" (*A Week*, 150).

The return to *Walden*, then, is really several returns superimposed on each other—the return of the 5-year-old to his infancy, to a state of oceanic oneness with nature and protective symbiosis with the mother; the return of the 28-year-old to that infancy through a replica-tion of this childhood visit; and the symbolic return of the race to its mythical paradise. The return in some ways reverses the effect of the Fall, the expulsion from paradise, just as the Europeans' return to what they perceived as the natural paradise of America held out the promise of redemption. Getting back in touch with the cyclic patterns of nature helps us experience the Fall as only temporary and reversible: as Thoreau says of the pines of Walden, "[I]f some have fallen, I have cooked my supper with their stumps, and a new growth is rising all around, preparing another aspect for new infant eyes." The statement is at one level a version of Emerson's "Infancy is the perpetual Messiah, which comes into the arms of fallen men, and pleads with them to return to paradise" (Emerson, 46). By taking the figures of the usually theological notions of the "fallen" and the "rising" with the kind of literalness that, as we have seen in the chapter 6, he reinfuses into common speech, Thoreau gives us a renaturalizing of religious myth, an etymology of belief.

A look at a passage from "The Ponds," which many critics see as a kind of mythical center to the book, will help us extend this notion:

> Successive nations perchance have drank at, admired, and fathomed it, and passed away, and still its water is green and pellucid as ever. Not an intermitting spring! Perhaps on that spring morning when Adam and Eve were driven out of Eden Walden Pond was already in existence, and even then breaking up in a gentle spring rain accompanied with mist and a southerly wind, and covered with myriads of ducks and geese, which had not heard of the fall, when still such pure lakes sufficed them. Even then it had commenced to rise and fall, and had clarified its waters and colored them of the hue they now wear, and obtained a patent of heaven to be the only Walden Pond in the world and distiller of celestial dews. Who knows in how many unremembered nations' literatures this has been the Castalian Fountain? or what nymphs presided over it in the Golden Age? It is a gem of the first water which Concord wears in her coronet.

(179)

The correlation between Eden and Walden is introduced effectively here by juxtaposing the two words. Because they belong to two different clauses, grammatically they should be separated by a comma, but their visual proximity and their rhyme sets up the metaphor: "Eden Walden Pond." A similar juxtaposition is at work in "spring morning"; at first hearing this seems a common-enough phrase, but it picks up and relates two patterns of imagery in the book, anticipating Thoreau's later equating the spring with the morning in his notion of the day epitomizing the year (303). And it is the interrelated series of puns on "spring" and "fall" that is at the wellspring of the passage. We know it was the season of spring when Adam and Eve were driven out of Eden, because it was always spring in Eden; the earth was not yet tilted on its axis, an act of God's vengeance that created the seasonal extremes of climate. And Walden is "not an intermitting spring," in both senses, just as it was described near the beginning of this chapter as "a perennial spring" (175). On the spring morning of the fall, the ducks and geese had not heard of the fall because there had never been one—only spring. But in a deeper sense Thoreau is finding a fresh way to state the romantic revision of Christianity—that nature did not fall when humans did. The ducks and geese are outside the circuit of law and language that regulates relations between the human and the divine. It is true that the pond changes according to its own cycles, to "rise and fall," but this circular rhythm is in contrast to the linear pattern of only one fall and one God-created possibility of redemption.

One of the more eccentric books on *Walden* suggests that there is a hidden Christian message, as emblematized by the fact that the two intersecting lines on Thoreau's map form an almost perfect cross.[3] If anything, the truth might lie in a sort of green magic inversion of this notion—that Christianity can be seen as an hardened and spiritualized version of Walden Pond in specific and of nature in general. One can see correlations among mythologies, not because of historical connections but because they ultimately derive from the same source, nature. Thoreau as mythographer equates the Judaeo-Christian Paradise with the classical Golden Age without giving either one priority: they both derive from the pure perennial "springs" of childhood, of morning, of the spinning seasons. As Ovid, whom Thoreau quotes later on this point (315–16), describes it, the Golden Age was a time before the fall, when there was no need of laws or prohibitions, and nature provided freely for her children. The season, of course, was always spring. One of the wonderful moments in *Walden* is when this archetype of the Golden Age, here seen as arising from nature itself, is once again concretized in the physical world at the end of "Spring": "The sulpher-like pollen of the pitch-pine soon covered the pond and the stones and rotten wood along the shore, so that you could have collected a barrel-ful. This is the 'sulphur showers' we hear of. Even in Calidas' drama of Sacontala, we read of 'rills dyed yellow with the golden dust of the lotus' " (319).

The "nymphs" mentioned in the passage are the property not so much of the Golden Age as of a related classical landscape, the pastoral. This is the landscape created by the Greek poet Theocritus in his *Idylls* and given its most definitive literary form by the Latin poet Virgil in the *Eclogues*. These poems created an ideal realm not at the beginning of time but in an extant geographic area, Arcadia, away from the complexities of urban life. Human shepherds lived a life of joy and authenticity, doing a kind of work that, like fishing, is often difficult to tell from idling. Virgil and his readers were aware that they were indulging in a sort of literary fantasy, that the real Arcadia in Greece was harsh and unsparing. With the discovery of America, though, the motifs and images of pastoralism took on new literal possibilities, especially when combined with the political and social vision of Jeffersonian agrarianism. The dream of rejoining the human to the natural in order to restore the lost garden seemed a likely candidate for realization (Marx, especially 242–65).

If we return to the beanfield passage, we can see how pastoral imagery is projected on to childhood reminiscences. What is usually called a "field" is called a "pasture," even though there is no evidence that herds ever grazed here. And while Thoreau did play a flute—it can be seen now in the Concord Historical Museum—his mention of it waking the echoes is a particularly pastoral motif, with the echoes suggesting a potential harmony and communication between the human and the natural. What Thoreau is doing here and in the entire book is clothing not only his own infant dreams but the fabulous landscape of the entire race, for the pastoral has essentially been an escape literature, a fantasy of retreat from all this now too much for us to a realm of simplicity and pleasure. Thoreau transforms it from a regressive revery to an active force, to direct work in the world.

In *Walden*, then, Thoreau analyzes a pining for the loss of his own childhood and transforms it into a more general mythography of the culture. To further relate some of the individual strands of this chapter, we can use the critic Northrop Frye's reading of romantic mythology:

> What corresponds to the older myth of an unfallen state, or lost paradise of Eden, is now a sense of an original identity between individual man and nature which has been lost. It may have been something lost in childhood, as in Wordsworth's *Ode on Intimations of Immortality*, or it may be somewhat hazier, like a racial collective memory, but it haunts the mind with the same sense of dispossession that the original Eden myth did. The context of what corresponds to the "fall," or the myth of alienation, changes accordingly. Man has "fallen," not so much into sin as into the original sin of self-consciousness, into his present subject-object relation to nature, where, because his consciousness is what separates him from nature, the primary conscious feeling is one of separation.[4]

The Walden experiment is more than an attempt at plain living and high thinking; it is an attempt to create structures that will make possible a reintegration of ourselves with the world, and of the mind with itself.

We have already seen how the sense of loss Frye mentions pervades the book, but we have yet to look at the most famous passage on the subject: "I long ago lost a hound, a bay horse, and a turtle-dove, and am still on their trail. Many are the travellers I have spoken concerning them, describing their tracks and what calls they answered to. I have met one or two who had heard the hound, and the tramp of the horse, and even seen the dove disappear behind a cloud, and they seemed as anxious to recover them as if they had lost them themselves" (17). In his notes to *The Variorum "Walden"* Walter Harding cites more sources on this than on any other passage, including an entire master's thesis.[5] Many of these sources try to read the passage as some hidden autobiography, about, for example, Thoreau's loss of Ellen Sewall. But the allusions here are no doubt intended to be as general and undefined as they are, for the passage is preceded in the text by these statements: "You will pardon some obscurities, for there are more secrets in my trade than in most men's, and yet not voluntarily kept, but inseparable from its very nature. I would gladly tell all that I know about it, and never paint 'No Admittance' on my gate" (17).

Although he is a Henry-of-all-trades, the particular trade here is that of a writer, a reviser of mythologies. When Thoreau said of this passage, "Why everybody has met with losses, have n't they?" (*Correspondence*, 479), he suggested that he was speaking to a shared sense of loss inherent in the very act of living. We, the audience to whom he speaks, are "travellers"—people without a home, or at least not at home now. He describes to us not the creatures themselves but "their tracks and what calls they answered to," and similarly we travellers have heard only the sounds of the animals as they run and hide or have seen them only in the act of disappearing—for the writer is in the paradoxical position of calling for this lost harmony in language, and language itself is the primary medium for the subject-object split Frye mentions. Thoreau wrote of the elusiveness of our infant dreams, "We linger in manhood to tell the dreams of our childhood, and they are half-forgotten ere we have learned the language" (*A Week*, 380). But it is at least partly our learning the language that makes these dreams recede ungraspably. One of the challenges Thoreau sets for himself in *Walden* is to "track" an experience that is essentially nonlinguistic, or is even antilinguistic, to find a language resonant and supple enough to transcend its own limitations as ordinary language, to find a language that can bridge subject and object instead of separating them.

We have already seen Thoreau do this in the first paragraph of

"Solitude," analyzed in chapter 6, through using the sounds and rhythms of the language itself. Significantly, the first sentence of the passage transforms two journal sentences—"The senses of children are unprofaned. Their whole body is one sense" (*Journal*, VI:111)—to "This is a delicious evening, when the whole body is one sense" (129). An infant will make sounds before she or he learns to speak, not for any extrinsic purpose but out of sheer erotic exuberance, out of the physical pleasure of the sounds themselves, and a writer like Thoreau can recapture this sense of joyful sound within language. What was a description of a seemingly lost childhood becomes an available adult experience, not only by waking earlier echoes but also by creating through language a receptivity to what can be called visionary consciousness.

This kind of consciousness restores an identity between ourselves and the world by making permeable, at least temporarily, those hard boundaries we draw around ourselves and between our conscious and unconscious. Probably the most famous description of it in American literature is Emerson's passage on the transparent eyeball: "Standing on the bare ground,—my head bathed by the blithe air, and uplifted into infinite space,—all mean egotism vanishes. I become a transparent eye-ball; I am nothing; I see all; the currents of the Universal Being circulate through me; I am part or particle of God" (Emerson, 10). Equivalent moments in *Walden* are less cosmic but involve no less an erasure between the self and the world, as when Thoreau finds identities shifting in his absorption of hoeing beans: "When my hoe tinkled against the stones, that music echoed to the woods and the sky, and was an accompaniment to my labor which yielded an instant and immeasurable crop. It was no longer beans that I hoed, nor I that hoed beans" (159). As in the paragraph from this chapter that we have already examined, the ecstasy—a word meaning literally standing outside oneself—is associated with echoing music and with physical labor. The feeling is more aural and tactile, more what we might call a whole-body experience, than in the Emerson passage. Further, while in Emerson the One often seems to be at odds with the Many, or at least to exist on a different plane of perception, in Thoreau's visionary consciousness, unity is more apt to be apprehended immediately through the multiplicity and diversity of the natural world. Right after the passage just quoted, Thoreau notices small birds, "graceful and slender like ripples caught up from the pond, as leaves are raised by the wind to float in the heavens; such kindredship is in Nature. The hawk is aerial brother of the wave which he sails over and surveys, those his perfect air-inflated wings answering to the elemental un-fledged pinions of the sea" (159).

Experiences and perceptions like these cannot be sought after too eagerly or directly, for to receive them we must renounce the notion of goal-directed behavior, of something to be attained for the future, and not "sacrifice the bloom of the present moment" (111). Further, this visionary consciousness requires abandoning the will to power over the external world and instead establishing a state of peaceful coexistence with it. Thoreau equates this stance with the Oriental "forsaking of works" (112), and says in the context of farming, "The true husbandman will cease from anxiety, as the squirrels manifest no concern whether the woods will bear chestnuts this year or not, and finish his labor with every day, relinquishing all claim to the produce of his fields, and sacrificing in his mind not only his first but his last fruits also" (166). Only with such an attitude can we leave behind the self that hoes beans only for profit. As one critic has described this consciousness in respect to modern poetry, "To walk barefoot into reality means abandoning the independence of the ego. Instead of making everything an object for the self, the mind must efface itself before reality, or plunge itself into the density of an exterior world, dispersing itself in a milieu which exceeds it and which it has not made."[6] What is called for is not a self-assertion in the face of nature but, rather, a self-abandonment, such as letting oneself be blown by the breezes in a small boat, or trusting like the squirrels that we will be fed.

Scholars have noted that, as *Walden* proceeds, the starchy ego of its speaker is less intrusive and insistent. What has been called the first person perpendicular[7] relaxes into an absorption with its surroundings. Thoreau seems to learn as the book goes on what he had stated more abstractly at the beginning: "We may waive just so much care of ourselves as we honestly bestow elsewhere" (11). If we are lucky enough to lose the construct of our adult selves, it is not a void we face; instead, we "*realize* where we are and the infinite extent of our relations" (171, emphasis added).

It is one of *Walden*'s triumphs that it takes that realm of infant pleasure and oceanic oneness with the world, and suggests we can rediscover it here and now. And we can rediscover it, not in some distant imaginative realm, out of space and out of time, as Poe posits, or in vast and mysterious ocean spaces, as Melville suggests, but in our small, daily alternations of work and rest, of words and silence. Thoreau wrote in 1841, "A slight sound at evening lifts me up by the ears—and makes life seem inexpressibly serene and grand" (*Journal*, 1:314) With this kind of attention and responsiveness, there is hope that the hound, bay horse, and turtledove may indeed be recaptured.

8

Philosophy
Heaven Can Wait

The title of this chapter may come as a surprise to the reader who has been following this volume so far, since one of its central points is that *Walden* cannot be reduced to a single outlook or set of propositions about the world. Its meanings reside, rather, in the rich, fluid, often unsettling experience of reading it, not in detachable statements suitable for sticking on buttons or bumpers. But while it is misleading to try to find a "philosophy" beyond or behind *Walden*'s structurings and languages, it will be helpful to conclude by showing how those structurings and languages delineate a series of stances toward the world that are, in the broadest sense, philosophical. Further, *Walden* is a book that reconsiders the whole enterprise of philosophy and the relation of that enterprise to the other aspects of our lives.

As mentioned in chapter 3, the contemporary reviewers did not feel uncomfortable in applying the word "philosophy" to the book, and Elizabeth Barstow Stoddard, writing in the *Daily Alta California*, even talked about his "philosophically matured vegetables." Indeed, most of the time "philosophy" and "philosophers" are used in *Walden* in a positive sense, as in the book's most famous pronouncement on the subject: "There are nowadays professors of philosophy, but not philosophers. Yet it is admirable to profess because it was once admirable to live. To be a philosopher is not merely to have subtle thoughts, nor even to found a school, but to so love wisdom as to live according to its dictates, a life of simplicity, independence, magnanimity, and trust. It is to solve some of the problems of life, not only theoretically, but practically" (14–15). Rarely has the technique discussed earlier of going to the roots of words been used more effectively. There are not only academic professors of philosophy but also people who profess a certain set of ideals without practicing them (the two groups are not exclusive of each other). More important, in going to the etymology of "philosophy" as "philos," love, + "sophia," wisdom, Thoreau has invoked a tradition that precedes the forming of schools, one that harkens back to the humility and the living out of personal conviction of Socrates, instead of to the metaphysical system building of Plato. And in the grammatical parallelism of this passage, "to live" is associated with philosophy. This stress on the "philos" as well as the "sophia" is characteristic not only of Thoreau but of the most vital and original strains in American philosophy. John Dewey, for example, was later to write, "We should return to the original and etymological sense of the word, and recognize that philosophy is a form of desire, of effort at action—a love, namely, of wisdom"[1] Dewey himself had not read Thoreau extensively, but presented with some of the latter's ideas, responded, "I am wondering why I have never gone to the source in his case. Has he been presented with too much austerity—as a kind of The Last Puritan?"[2]

This convergence with Dewey is significant, however, because it allows us to see Thoreau not just as an eccentric or homespun thinker but as an important figure in the most powerful channel of American philosophy. It is a profoundly antitraditional tradition of thought that stretches from the earliest European settlers, from Emerson to William James and John Dewey through Wallace Stevens and Robert Frost to Richard Rorty. Thoreau is a kind of pivot between transcendentalism and what came to be known as pragmatism, which, put simply, is a way of thinking that devalues traditional abstract philosophy, with its system building, only to value other things more: one's immediate experience in the world, the mind's ability to make meanings of that experience from moment to moment independent of rigid formulations from the past, and a disposition to turn these meanings back into significant action. Pragmatism sees knowledge as something not so much discovered as made or constructed, such as a house or a poem, and it stresses other modes, besides knowledge, of relating to the world, such as love and participation. It is concerned more with process than with any specific products, concerned more with an immediate responsiveness to life than with any single intellectual approach: "No method nor discipline can supersede the necessity of being forever on the alert" (111).

In the spirit of this tradition we should not try to delineate it here further in general terms; instead, we should locate ourselves in the text to see if we can apprehend it in its very turns of thought and language. The chapter "The Pond in Winter" begins with Thoreau apparently waking, but troubled by a kind of mental muffling and blurring:

> After a still winter night I awoke with the impression that some question had been put to me, which I had been endeavoring in vain to answer in my sleep, as what—how—when—where? But there was dawning Nature, in whom all creatures live, looking in at my broad windows with serene and satisfied face, and no question on *her* lips. I awoke to an answered question, to Nature and daylight. The snow lying deep on the earth dotted with young pines, and the very slope of the hill on which my house is placed, seemed to say Forward! Nature puts no question and answers none which we mortals ask. She has long ago taken her resolution.
>
> (283)

The meandering movement of the first sentence suggests a mind thick with cobwebs. "Still" most obviously means "quiet," but it also suggests that for the mind it *remains* night, even though the sun is rising. The preponderance and increased clustering of prepositions and other structuring words ("After ... with ... that ... to ... which ... in ... to ... in") turns into a string of vague, detached interrogative adverbs ("what—how—when—where?") giving a sense of the mind floating without an anchor, caught in its own convolutions. The "But" beginning the next sentence turns the meaning sharply, and the repetition of "l" and "s" sounds ("a*ll* . . . *l*ive . . . *l*ooking . . . window*s* . . . *s*erene . . . *s*atisfied . . . face . . . que*s*tion" culminate crisply in "*l*ips). The third sentence begins by echoing the words "I awoke" from the first sentence, but the cleaner, clearer rhythm and syntax suggest that this awakening is complete, not just physiological. This more inclusive sense of awakening links the passage to one of the motifs that pervades the book from the opening epigraph about awakening neighbors to the closing sentences about seeing the sun as but a morning star. More specifically, this awakening invokes the earlier sentence, "Every man has to learn the points of compass again as often as he awakes, whether from sleep or any abstraction (171)," for Thoreau is here doing both, as questions so abstract that they have no particular subjects or objects are dispelled in the bracing morning light. The fully awakened mind now meets nature as a dynamic, energizing force, as it connects the dotted trees with its own directional arrow and follows the gravitational nudge out of the house and toward the pond. Nature is viewed in a curiously balanced way. It is personified as feminine, looking in at windows and having lips, yet does not and will not speak our language; it is vaguely but pervasively nurturing—"in whom all creatures live"—yet is also mysteriously elusive and aloof.

Instead of viewing the landscape through the frame of his window, like a spectator viewing a "still" life, Thoreau now puts his body as well as his mind into the landscape to create yet another kind of window:

> Then to my morning work. First I take an axe and pail and go in search of water, if that be not a dream. After a cold and snowy night it needed a divining rod to find it. . . . Standing on the snow-covered plain, as if in a pasture amid the hills, I cut my way first through a foot of snow, and then a foot of ice, and open a window under my feet, where, kneeling to drink, I look down into the quiet parlor of the fishes, pervaded by a softened light as through a window of ground glass, with its bright sanded floor the same as in summer; there a perennial waveless serenity reigns, as in the amber

twilight sky, corresponding to the cool and even temperament of the inhabitants. Heaven is under our feet as well as over our heads.

(282–83)

The five words of the simple first sentence might seem routine, but the phrase "morning work," like the related notion of "awakening," has been charged with significance in the early chapters, as in this: "Morning work! By the blushes of Aurora and the music of Memnon, what should be man's *morning work* in this world?" (36). The question has become rhetorical: morning work is not simply work done in the morning but work that releases the mind to ever-fresh vision. The three words ending this last quotation could as well be emphasized as the two before it, for such restoring work can be done only *in this world*, not in some distant or imaginary one. As Thoreau will say in the last chapter, "How long shall we sit in our porticoes practising idle and musty virtues, which any work would make impertinent? As if one were to begin the day with long-suffering and hire a man to hoe his potatoes; and in the afternoon go forth to practise Christian meekness and charity with goodness aforethought!" (331).

As the movement of this passage suggests, the purity of Thoreau's vision is intertwined with, rather than cleaved from, the body and its routine physical activities. Along with Walt Whitman and Robert Frost, Thoreau is our great singer of work, not for any extrinsic values, such as economics or the Puritan ethic, but for its sheer rhythmic and muscular joys. In "House-Warming" he looks on his woodpile affectionately, with "the more chips the better to remind me of my pleasing work" (251). Although for others, "pleasing work" would be an oxymoron, some of Thoreau's physical pleasure in work is conveyed here in the strings of monosyllables and in the emphasis on sequence: "First I take an axe and pail and go in search of water, if that be not a dream. . . . I cut my way first through a foot of snow, and then a foot of ice," as if each word itself is a stride or a stroke of the ax biting the ice. The repetitions of "first" and "foot" and the way each of these echoes the other with the same initial and ending sounds simulate the repetitive yet satisfying actions. Thoreau comes to learn here that the always fresh and inspiring Walden water is not a dream but the boon of work in the same way Frost's mower learns that "the fact is the sweetest dream that labor knows."

The finding of water itself, though, is not a surprise; what is, is that this glimpse of Walden through the ice can be as quickening and as full of awe as the entire pond was before freezing. It is more precious for having to be earned in this way, yet more delightful for not having been directly sought. This and more are registered in the symmetrically balanced last sentence, which falls neatly into mirroring halves:

> Heaven is under our feet
> as well as over our heads.

This is the kind of aphorism that can quickly become banal on a greeting card; in its muted context, however, it maintains its vibrancy. "Feet," for example, has a particularly keen reverberation coming after the "foot" of snow and then the "foot" of ice. Its brevity and the simplicity of its diction take on a crystallizing and epitomizing quality after the complex and Latinate sentence before it.

The rhythmic and syntactic balance here suggest an equivalence between earth and heaven, below and above, body and mind that questions the hierarchical relationship that traditional religion and philosophy erect between the pairs. There is also a word play on "over our heads," in the sense of beyond our comprehension, that tells us that while heaven may be partly beyond our grasp it is still partly within our reach. The sentence culminates not only these first two paragraphs of its chapter but a series of previous images and statements, such as the book's shortest sentence: "Sky water" (188). This "sky water" can often be found under our feet, even in the midst of another winter routine, as Thoreau describes the tracks of winter walks: "For a week of even weather I took exactly the same number of steps, and of the same length, coming and going, stepping deliberately and with the precision of a pair of dividers in my own deep tracks,—to such routine the winter reduces us,—yet often they were filled with heaven's own blue" (265). The sentence also gathers up scattered images and pronouncements as in: "Olympus is but the outside of the earth every where" (85); "I would drink deeper, fish in the sky whose bottom is pebbly with stars" (98); and "Talk of heaven! ye disgrace earth" (200). In remembering his talks with the philosopher of "Winter Visitors," Thoreau says, "Whichever way we turned, it seemed that the heavens and the earth had met together" (269). And we can see now that Walden is "God's Drop" (194), not only in the sense of its heavenly beauty but also because it represents a descent, or "drop," of God himself to earth, an amalgam of Christ and Icarus.

This repositioning of heaven turns back on its immediate context to give more resonance to words like "divining" and "kneeling." The divining rod here finds divinity as well as water and is now more clearly linked to the visionary one mentioned earlier: "I think that the richest vein is somewhere hereabouts; so by the divining rod and thin rising vapors I judge; and here I will begin to mine" (98). "Kneeling" in this context takes on the implications Emerson used when he spoke of those who "see prayer in all action. The prayer of the farmer kneeling in his field to weed it, the prayer of the rower kneeling with the stroke of his oar" (Emerson, 276). And the drinking of water becomes a kind of secular communion, both a necessary of life and another chance to imbibe delight through every pore.

We must be careful, though, not to weigh this passage down with too much religious symbology and so make it more traditional and orthodox than it is. The religious overtones are used not to suggest a far-off realm of the spirit, but rather to turn their sanctifying aura back to our immediate life in nature. The water of the pond, "the same as in summer," and "the amber twilight sky" may mirror each other, just as in the later epiphany of spring we see it "reflecting a summer evening sky in its bosom, though none was visible overhead" (312). But if they symbolize anything beyond themselves it is an immediate inner state of quiet joy. Similarly, "perennial" carries a sense of the eternal but is, significantly, applied to a potable, fluid realm threaded with the movement of fish, as opposed to the hard, static, dormant covering of ice. Moreover, the "serenity" of the pond is based on not only its wavelessness but also its constant change, like the shifting shades of the twilight sky.

It is the word "heaven," though, that is used most dramatically and effectively in this way and is the hinge of this passage, for Thoreau not only draws on the fact that the word means at once our own sky and some imagined hereafter, some meta-physical home of God, but even has a theory as to how the former came to be corrupted into the latter: "When the common man looks into the sky, which he has not so much profaned, he thinks it less gross than the earth, and with reverence speaks of 'The Heavens,' but the seer will in the same sense speak of 'The Earths' " (*A Week*, 382). Just as we have seen that Thoreau's general linguistic strategy is to restore the original concrete force of abstract words, so here particularly he wants to reinvest our physical earth and heaven with the original reverence we felt for them, instead of misplacing it on their dim religious projections. This passage from *A Week* also says, "We need pray for no higher heaven than the pure senses can furnish, a *purely* sensuous life. . . . May we not *see* God? Are we to be put off and amused in this life, as it were mere allegory? Is not Nature, rightly read, that of which she is commonly taken to be the symbol merely?" (*A Week*, 382). And even more succinctly, two pages earlier Thoreau says, "Here or nowhere is our heaven" (*A Week*, 380). Although *Walden* contains less explicit delineation of this stance, more of it is registered, as I have tried to show, in the very texture and rhythms of the prose. Almost every page incarnates the notion Thoreau puts into a couplet in "The Ponds": "I cannot come nearer to God and Heaven / Than I live to Walden even" (193).

We see in these first two paragraphs of "The Pond in Winter" a characteristically American movement of mind that Emerson described as follows: "Whilst the abstract question occupies your intellect, nature brings it in the concrete to be solved by your hands" (Emerson, 48). The active, restless mind, frequently troubled by philosophical questions, finds that in going about one's business in the world these questions either dissolve or are answered in ways one could scarcely have anticipated. In Ernest Hemingway's *The Sun Also Rises* the protagonist, Jake Barnes, is also troubled in the night by such questions and, in an attempt to allay them, spins out a philosophy of life based on economic metaphors—a philosophy he immediately turns on and critiques: "In five years, I thought, it will seem just as silly as all the other philosophies I've had. . . . Perhaps as you went along you did learn something. I did not care what it was all about. All I wanted to know was how to live in it. Maybe if you found out how to live in it you learned from that what it was all about."[3]

Some such hypothesis, though hardly articulated or drawn up as a specific strategy, helps shape the arc of the entire Walden experiment. Thoreau begins by laying the economic foundations of a life that will allow him the most time for thinking, writing, discovering spirit, and observing nature, and finds that many of the benefits he expects from these activities come in the arranging itself: "I had this advantage, at least, in my mode of life, over those who were obliged to look abroad for amusement, to society and the theatre, that my life itself was become my amusement and never ceased to be novel" (112). Of all previous practices and creeds, probably the closest to this vision is Zen Buddhism, and its teachings were not yet available to Thoreau. But as we shall soon see, if Thoreau needed any traditions for precedent and support, these were available in certain indigenous American strains.

As we turn to the rest of "The Ponds in Winter," we can see that this issue of how best to live in the world and the relation of this living to knowing form a central theme, or leitmotif. Particularly in these later chapters there is a kind of tension or counterpoint between a more narrative organization—recounting or re-creating the events of a certain period—and a more topical one, so that the "subject" of this chapter is not as clear as it is in, say, "Solitude." But it is here in an almost subliminal way. For example, after Thoreau depicts his own task on the ice, arrive fishermen, who also delve beneath the surface for their work. On one level the movement is chronological in terms of a typical day's events, since even these early worms arrive later than Thoreau, who lives by the pond. But more significantly, on a thematic level they represent a life even deeper in nature than Thoreau's had become and reenact daily his own discovery of a formerly hidden heaven.

These fishers are "wild men, who instinctively follow other fashions and trust other authorities than their townsmen, . . . as wise in natural lore as the citizen is in artificial. They never consulted with books, and know and can tell much less than they have done. The things which they practise are said not yet to be known" (283). The "other authorities" are really their own interactions with nature, a direct, experiential grasp of the world that is not yet conceptualized or even verbalized. It is, rather, something embodied and lived out. These mute, inglorious Waltons are capable of producing results even more awesome and startling than Thoreau's finding a summer firmament under the Walden ice: "Here is one fishing for pickerel with grown perch for bait. You look into his pail with wonder as into a summer pond, as if he kept summer locked up at home, or knew where she had retreated" (283). Unlike John Field, who tries to catch perch with shiners, "thinking to live by some derivative old country mode in this primitive new country" (208), this man knows some native secrets: "O, he got worms out of rotten logs since the ground froze, and so he caught them" (283).

With these worms, then, he catches perch to catch pickerel from under the ice, which Thoreau presents as an analogue to his own discovery of heaven beneath: "Ah, the pickerel of Walden! when I see them lying on the ice, or in the well which the fisherman cuts in the ice, making a little hole to admit the water, I am always surprised by their rare beauty, as if they were fabulous fishes, they are so foreign to the streets, even to the woods, foreign as Arabia to our Concord life. They possess a quite dazzling and transcendent beauty" (284). True to the vision of a book where heaven is underfoot, this is the only place where the adjectives "dazzling" and "transcendent" appear. The fish are common in the sense of plentiful, yet they are also "rare" and "fabulous," and Thoreau has the remarkable capacity to be "always surprised" by them. Later in the paragraph he will note once more, "It is surprising that they are caught here" (284). This capacity to find the miraculous in the commonplace and to never take it for granted is what gives so much of the prose here and elsewhere its sheen. At the end of this paragraph we see a pickerel die on the surface "like a mortal translated before his time to the thin air of heaven" (285), perhaps an incipient parallel to what might happen to us if we got our Sunday wishes for a higher heaven, suggesting that, both for the pickerel and for us, Heaven is here at Walden or nowhere.

The chapter goes on to consider various ways the pond is known and not known. Thoreau's own survey of the pond's bottom debunks the myth that the pond is bottomless. Having done that debunking, however, now gives him the right to say, "I am thankful that this pond was made deep and pure for a symbol. While men believe in the infinite some ponds will be thought to be bottomless" (287). This statement is not as contradictory or confusing as some have made it out to be, if we remember Thoreau's attitude toward symbol making—that is, ideas should be rendered through metaphor in concrete, tangible forms, so that even notions of infinity and eternity are metaphorically expressed through temporal and limited objects. The paradox is the same as Hart Crane calling the sea "this great wink of eternity," with the wink acknowledging the sea's temporal nature even as it stands as an emblem for the eternal. As Thoreau takes his soundings, he discovers—quite serendipitously, as he presents it—that the line of greatest length intersects with the line of greatest breadth at the greatest depth. He goes on to explore the moral and ethical truths suggested by this fact, but as with using the pond for a symbol for the infinite, he does not confound the two realms but remains quite deliberately aware of his symbolizing process.

Next comes a long description of the ice cutters who came to the pond in the winter of 1846–47. Unlike Thoreau or the ice fishermen, they cut through the ice not for the immediate needs of thirst or hunger but for the more remote, almost abstract ones of selling it in the summer for a businessman "who is impressively, even pathetically wise, to foresee the heat and thirst of July now in January" (294). This man is out of synch with the seasons; unlike Thoreau and the fishermen, he does not merely make windows in the ice but, rather, "unroofs the house of fishes and carts off their element and air (294)," trying vainly to remove the fish's heaven, since much of the ice is left to melt by the shore. Like the railroad in the "Sounds" chapter, the ice cutters are treated with a kind of playful, mock-heroic language that displays the ambivalence Thoreau feels toward both enterprises. The pond is being needlessly and, it turns out, ineffectively despoiled, and yet the fate of the Walden water that is shipped to farther and hotter climes captures Thoreau's imagination in the famous last paragraph of the chapter:

Thus it appears that the sweltering inhabitants of Charleston and New Orleans, of Madras and Bombay and Calcutta, drink at my well. In the morning I bathe my intellect in the stupendous and cosmogonal philosophy of the Bhagvat Geeta, since whose composition years of the gods have elapsed, and in comparison with which our modern world and its literature seem puny and trivial; and I doubt if that philosophy is not to be referred to a previous state of existence, so remote is its sublimity from our conceptions. I lay down the book and go to my well for water, and lo! there I meet the servant of the Brahmin, priest of Brahma and Vishnu and Indra, who still sits in his temple on the Ganges reading the Vedas, or dwells at the root of a tree with his crust and his jug. I meet his servant come to draw water for his master, and our buckets as it were grate together in the same well. The pure Walden water is mingled with the sacred water of the Ganges. With favoring winds it is wafted past the site of the fabulous islands of Atlantis and the Hesperides, makes the periplus of Hanno, and, floating by Ternate and Tidore and the mouth of the Persian Gulf, melts in the tropic gales of the Indian seas, and is landed in ports of which Alexander only heard the names.

(297–98)

The paragraph is often quoted for its rhapsodic qualities, but it is particularly important here for broadening the implications of the chapter's opening scenes. From several earlier passages—Thoreau's sitting in his doorway in "Sounds," for example, or the fable about the artist of Kouroo—Oriental religions evoke a state of meditation that puts one outside of time. But while these passages have generally been positive, one notices that here the Oriental experience envisioned is curiously bifurcated: that while Thoreau puts down his book and goes to the well himself, the Brahmin "still sits . . . reading the Vedas"—reminding one of those flesh-mortifying Brahmins at the very beginning who sit "chained for life at the foot of a tree" (4)—and sends his servant for water. As we reflect further, the opening references to Charleston and New Orleans, two of the major slave markets in this country, become more than just vaguely southern place-names.

It is not that the Oriental vision is weighed and discarded, but, rather, that for all its imaginative cosmic sweep in space and time, some crucial earthly things are omitted. To talk of a religious vision

111

as "remote" is not completely positive in a book that also says, "Men esteem truth remote, in the outskirts of the system. . . . But all these times and places and occasions are now and here. God himself culminates in the present moment" (96–97). Of all the Eastern texts available to him, Thoreau especially valued the Bhagvat Geeta for its attempt to reconcile the life of action with that of contemplation. But just as Thoreau liberally stirs into *Walden* generous portions from Oriental scriptures, as in the first paragraph of "The Pond in Winter," so should the process become reciprocal: the Orient could learn from Thoreau's immersion in the exigencies and self-sufficiency of a frontier American life. Atlantis and the Hesperides are indeed "fabulous," but no more so than the pickerel of Walden, as we have just seen. This last paragraph provides answers to a question in the earlier satiric dialogue between Poet and Hermit, wherein the latter, sitting in meditation on "these three sentences of Con-fut-see," wonders, "Shall I go to heaven or a-fishing?" (224). The entire chapter suggests how they can be one and the same. Indeed, the satire of the dialogue is directed at the hermit, who can fool himself and his friend into thinking that meditation is a higher state than digging for worms. The ice fishers here know differently.

We can now extend some of the implications of "The Pond in Winter" to the entire Walden experiment. When Thoreau says early in the book, "It would be some advantage to live a primitive and frontier life, though in the midst of an outward civilization" (11), he is referring primarily to what he calls the arrangement of our "outward condition or circumstances" (4). But as the book proceeds, this apparent act of atavism becomes much more concerned with how we relate to the world in terms of our immediate consciousness. The frontiers become less those of economic survival and more those of perception and experience. With the kind of etymological wordplay we have seen so often, Thoreau links the notion of the physical frontier with the act of confronting, or "fronting" the new: "The frontiers are not east or west, north or south, but wherever a man *fronts* a fact, though that fact be his neighbor, there is an unsettled wilderness between him and Canada, between him and the setting sun, or, further still, between him and *it*. Let him build himself a log-house with the bark on where he is, *fronting* IT, and wage there an Old French war for seven or seventy years, with Indians and Rangers, or whatever else may come between him and the reality, and save his scalp if he can" (*A Week*, 304). In *Walden*, of course, Thoreau, a descendant from old French stock, does build himself a house of logs hewn only on one or two sides, "leaving the rest of the bark on" (42), "to front only the essential facts of life" (90). The challenge is to clear or "settle" that unsettled wilderness between him and reality—a reality that, like the setting sun, is itself always in motion, always westering, always about to go under the horizon—so that it can best be apprehended. As Joan Burbick has shown,[4] Thoreau self-consciously and deliberately puts himself in the role of a "settler," as opposed to his role in previous works as simply a traveler, to have access to those aspects of nature which are revealed only to such a one. "How much, what infinite leisure it requires, as of a lifetime, to appreciate a single phenomenon! You must camp down beside it as for life, having reached your land of promise, and give yourself wholly to it" (*Journal*, IV:433). Thoreau replicates in microcosm the position of first occupant of a New World to constantly track the mind's perennial encounter with newness: "How novel and original must be each new man's view of the universe! for though the world is so old, and so many books have been written, each object appears wholly undescribed to our experience, each field of thought wholly unexplored. The whole world is an America, a *New World*" (*Journal*, III:384).

America presents not only new opportunities for meeting the exigencies of our lives but, through those opportunities, new ways of relating to the world. Thoreau sensed these opportunities in ways that historians and philosophers have only recently been articulating, as has Daniel Boorstin in *The Americans: The Colonial Experience*:

> The haze which covered the New World in that age probably covers no part of the world today; America was one of the last places where European settlers would come in large numbers *before* the explorers, geographers, and professional naturalists. With little

more than hearsay and advertising to guide them, early Americans had many of the joys and tasks, the surprises and disappointments of explorers though they lived the lives of permanent settlers. This was a crucial fact; it would brighten their thinking about the world around them; it would affect their ideal of man; it would liberate them from many of the metaphysical and dogmatic problems which plagued the more introspective, library-oriented man of Europe; it would entice their eyes and minds to varied, shifting, unpredictable shapes of the world around them—shapes on which every man, sometimes the first viewer, was his own authority. The time had come for the overcultivated man of Europe to rediscover the earth on which he walked. . . . We sometimes forget how gradual was the "discovery" of America; it was a by-product of the *occupation* of the continent. To act, to move on, to explore meant also to push back the frontiers of knowledge; this inevitably gave a practical and dynamic character to the very idea of knowledge. To learn and to act became one.[5]

With these ideas in mind, we can see more clearly the ways in which Thoreau fuses into one those archetypal American roles of explorer and settler. As we have seen in "The Pond in Winter," to work in the world is to come to know it. The fishermen, "who know and can tell much less than they have done" (283), have at least the potential for genuine knowing and telling because their fronting of reality has been so immediate and authentic, whereas those who try to relate to the *New* World with preconceptions or already-established systems will always be insulated from it. And significantly, it is in the chapter titled "Higher Laws" that Thoreau says, "Fishermen, hunters, woodchoppers, and others, spending their lives in the fields and woods, in a peculiar sense a part of Nature themselves, are often in a more favorable mood for observing her, in the intervals of their pursuits, than philosophers or poets even, who approach her with expectation" (210).

And so Thoreau, himself a quondam and future philosopher and poet, tries to purge himself of expectation by starting again literally from the ground up, furnishing all his needs "by the labor of my hands only" (1). He tries to actually live from the inside what has become a cultural and literary stereotype, one to which he refers with some self-irony as "a very *agricola laboriosus* . . . I the homestaying, laborious native of the soil" (157):

> Meanwhile my beans, the length of whose rows, added to-gether, was seven miles already planted, were impatient to be hoed, for the earliest had grown considerably before the latest were in the ground; indeed they were not easily to be put off. What was the meaning of this so steady and self-respecting, this small Herculean labor, I knew not. I came to love my rows, my beans, though so many more than I wanted. They attached me to the earth, and so I got strength like Antaeus. But why should I raise them? Only Heaven knows. This was my curious labor all summer long, to make this portion of the earth's surface, which had yielded only cinquefoil, blackberries, johnswort, and the like, before, sweet wild fruits and pleasant flowers, produce, instead this pulse. What shall I learn of beans or beans of me? I cherish them, I hoe them, early and late I have an eye to them; and this is my day's work.
>
> (155)

"Meanwhile" is a wonderfully appropriate way to begin this chapter on "The Bean-Field," since it suggests that while we talk and write on, nature, even when we ourselves channel it, goes at its own indepen-dent pace and challenges us to keep up with it. The growth of Tho-reau's beans are almost an intrusion on his mental life, like the later tug at his fishing line "which came to interrupt your dreams and link you to Nature again" (175). This opening is a more concrete version of Emerson's first sentence in "Experience": "Where do we find our-selves?" (Emerson, 471). His answer, as Thoreau's also seems to be here, is always in the middle of something, not quite sure of how we got into it all and uncertain of where it will all lead. We do not so much carefully chart our actions or our lives and then fulfill that plan as we find ourselves at work and in that process prod it for meaning. Thoreau's syntactic version of this idea is a kind of double interroga-tive, a sentence that starts out as a question but is followed by a confession of no answer: "What was the meaning of this so steady and self-respecting, this small Herculean labor, I knew not" (155).

Three more sentences in this paragraph are direct questions, and another—"Only heaven knows"—is one more quizzical shrug. This sense of not knowing what to make of it all is also registered in the modifiers of "labor": "curious" and "small Herculean." The latter would seem to be oxymoronic, since any labor like Hercules's should be mighty. Perhaps Thoreau is trying to differentiate his labor here from that of his townspeople, whose own labors are unlike Hercules's because they are endless.

In any case, meanings seem to emerge if we lean on the resonances of words rather than on explicit propositions, just as the activity itself starts to be intrinsically rewarding without fulfilling any larger metaphysical or economic goals. The renewals of strength Thoreau experiences are similar to the way he and his poet friend in "House-Warming" sharpen and shine their knives, "by thrusting them into the earth" (241). The beans "attach" Thoreau to the earth first in a physical way, as his hoe connects him almost umbilically to the soil, and then in forming an affectionate bond—"I came to love my beans," "I cherish them." Although the terms here may seem excessive to the point of comic irony, there is a genuine satisfaction both in the ordering, nurturing nature of the activity and in the rhythmic, muscular exertion Thoreau also enjoys in chopping ice, rowing, swimming. Since like Antaeus he gets strength through this contact, he is right to ask why he should then "raise"—also in the sense of "lift up"—the beans, where they too will lose their strength and eventually their lives as plants as they are picked.

If Thoreau came to love his beans, why the questionings here, why the misgivings? These arise from what the neat, straight rows of beans displace: "But what right had I to oust johnswort and the rest, and break up their ancient herb garden?" (155). Thoreau finds himself situated at the very cutting edge between the wild and the cultivated, the unknown and the known, which, as we shall see later in this chapter, affords the best vantage to apprehend the world. But there are dangers on both sides of the line, as rendered in comic mismatches between language and action. When Thoreau says, "Daily the beans saw me come to their rescue armed with a hoe, and thin the ranks of their enemies, filling up the trenches with weedy dead" (161), the humor comes from overcultivating the situation, using a language too pretentious because it is too anthropomorphic. On the other hand, to know beans just as beans is indeed to know very little, to know beans indeed; it is to be too restricted to the level of literal concreteness and simplicity that the Canadian woodchopper is, when he cannot "get" the metaphor of Plato's definition of man as a featherless biped.

Thoreau's query as to what he shall learn of beans turns later in the chapter into one of his most famous puns: "I was determined to know beans." Like Ishmael's determination to know whales, the inquiry becomes a synecdoche for the question of how well we can know the natural that lies outside the human universe, the Isle of Man. And like Ishmael's quest, it seems to meet with as little ultimate success, no matter how entertaining and revealing the pursuit itself is. We have already seen in chapter 6 the variety of languages Thoreau uses in "The Bean-Field"; they all seem to approach the reality of raising beans asymptotically, never quite approaching their object. What one critic has written of Ishmael in *Moby-Dick* is equally relevant here: "The mind that moved out to incorporate the world turns back on itself and becomes self-conscious about its own procedures, discovering that the sense it had made of its objects is not that of objective fact but of a self-contained mental construct. And at the same moment that Ishmael understands the fictiveness of thought he comes to see the world as 'full of strangeness,' with a renewed sense of its final impenetrable mystery."[6] This perspective helps explain the otherwise-puzzling epic Thoreau creates of himself as a Greek warrior battling Trojan weeds. It is typical of our need for making fictions out of our lives, for self-dramatization, even when we are not sure what we are doing or why we are doing it.

We must, then, take Thoreau's pun seriously. Perhaps his relation to beans might be more authentic by knowing little about them, by knowing just beans about beans, even by unknowing. There are other ways of relating to the world aside from "knowing" it, and this is where Thoreau in particular and American philosophy in general is most revisionary. Throughout its modern history, philosophy has centered on a series of problems that are primarily epistemological, focusing on a subject, the knower, and an object, the world. Locke, for example, assigned more weight to the latter than the former, and the German idealists reversed his formulation, but both were concerned with the same dynamic. Thoreau, however, despite his intense curiosity, did not see the relationship between self and the world exclusively or even primarily as that of knower to known. He elaborates on his view most explicitly in "Walking," a lecture he gave frequently when he was in the last stages of finishing *Walden*: "My desire for knowledge is intermittent, but my desire to bathe my head in atmospheres unknown to my feet is perennial and constant. The highest that we can attain to is not Knowledge, but Sympathy and Intelligence. I do not know that this higher knowledge amounts to anything more definite than a novel and grand surprise or a sudden revelation of the insufficiency of all that we called Knowledge before,—a discovery that there are more things in heaven and earth than are dreamed of in our philosophy" (*Natural*, 128). Freud said we can know the psychologically healthy person by his or her ability to do two things, to work and to love, and Thoreau comes to know his beans through both modes. His labor in the beanfield gives him the kind of more embracing and more intimate knowledge that he finds in the ice fisher: "His life passes deeper in Nature than the studies of the naturalist penetrate; himself a subject for the naturalist. The latter raises the moss and bark gently with his knife in search of insects; the former lays open logs to their core with his axe, and moss and bark fly far and wide. He gets his living by barking trees" (283). The naturalist seems to be engaged in only mild foreplay, as opposed to the fisherman, who will "penetrate" further. And by this point in the book we have been thoroughly sensitized for the pun in "gets his living."

But Thoreau's counterepistemology includes more than work and love, as we see in the last sentence from "Walking," which appropriately begins, "I do not know," for Thoreau is talking not about knowing but about feeling for the limits of one's knowledge, a process that necessarily cannot be fully known or articulated. It can, though, help us come closer to the initially puzzling statement near the beginning of *Walden*: "How can he remember well his ignorance—which his growth requires—who has so often to use his knowledge?" (6). Knowledge helps us map out the world and function in it, but after a while we come to mistake the map for the territory and blind ourselves to what is not on it. Custom and habit take over instead of immediate apprehension of what is always new, always changing. It is in those moments when we let ourselves encounter something not on the map, not previously charted and articulated, that we truly learn.

As Thoreau says in "The Village" about the terrain that lies between the village and his pondside settlement,

> It is a surprising and memorable, as well as valuable experience, to be lost in the woods any time. Often in a snow-storm, even by day, one will come out upon a well-known road, and yet find it impossible to tell which way leads to the village. Though he knows that he has travelled it a thousand times, he cannot recognize a feature in it, but it is as strange to him as if it were a road in Siberia. By night, of course, the perplexity is infinitely greater. In our most trivial walks, we are constantly, though unconsciously, steering like pilots by certain well-known beacons and headlands, and if we go beyond our usual course we still carry in our minds the bearing of some neighboring cape; and not till we are completely lost, or turned round,—for a man needs only to be turned round once with his eyes shut in this world to be lost,—do we appreciate the vastness and strangeness of Nature. Every man has to learn the points of the compass again as often as he awakes, whether from sleep or any abstraction. Not till we are lost, in other words, not till we have lost the world, do we begin to find ourselves, and realize where we are and the infinite extent of our relations.
>
> (170–71)

"Surprising," "memorable," "valuable"—all are in apposition, since being "always surprised" is not just pleasurable but keeps one on this edge of awareness. Snow, night, dizziness—anything that forces us to abandon our old knowledge in favor of new experience—is valuable.

This is one reason seasonal change, even that of winter, is so important in the book. "Winter Animals" begins, "When the ponds were firmly frozen, they afforded not only new and shorter routes to many points, but new views from their surfaces of the familiar landscape around them" (270). For *Walden*'s contemporary readers, "new views" was a phrase commonly used for transcendentalism in general, taken from an 1836 pamphlet *New Views of Christianity, Society, and the Church*, by Orestes Brownson, with whom Thoreau lived and studied German for a few months. While retaining this resonance, though, "new views" here is very concrete, giving us a new apprehension of the physical world. It is a specific example of the sentence in "Conclusion" that says, "The universe is wider than our views of it" (320). *Walden* is like the series paintings of Monet; no single view of the woods, the pond, is the truth, but each new view can be a wider glimpse of both perceived and perceiver. Thoreau relishes those moments when our old views—be they mental paradigms, self-concepts, or visual perspectives—dissolve into the newness before them: "The wisely conscious life springs out of an unconscious suggestion. . . . Indeed, it is by obeying the suggestions of a higher light within you that you escape from yourself and, in the transit, as it were see with the unworn sides of your eye, travel totally new paths" (*Journal*, IX:37–38).

All this helps answer a question that has been asked from the first reviewers on: why does Thoreau leave Walden? Years later, when he was a sojourner in civilized life again, he himself often wondered why. But the book itself speaks to the questions in two different places. At the end of "Spring," which marks the end of the chronological narrative, there is a stark two-sentence paragraph: "Thus was my first year's life in the woods completed; and the second year was similar to it. I finally left Walden September 6th, 1847" (319). And in the subsequent "Conclusion" there is this:

> I left the woods for as good a reason as I went there. Perhaps it seemed to me that I had several more lives to live, and could not spare any more time for that one. It is remarkable how easily and insensibly we fall into a particular route, and make a beaten track for ourselves. I had not lived there a week before my feet wore a path from my door to the pond-side; and though it is five or six years since I trod it, it is still quite distinct. It is true, I fear that

others may have fallen into it, and so helped to keep it open. The surface of the earth is soft and impressible by the feet of men; and so with the paths which the mind travels.

(323)

Both answers are implicit in each other. Even this new, fresh life began to repeat, to copy itself the second year. As Emerson wrote, "Every thought is also a prison; every heaven is also a prison" (Emerson, 463). The very predictability Thoreau sought in observing the seasons, in sounding the pond, sapped the vitality from perceiving them. In these last two chapters, exuberantly upbeat as they are, is a poignant undercurrent from the inevitable difficulty of enacting any such experiment, for the very acts of settling and knowing defeat the deep psychological springs from which those acts arose: "At the same time that we are earnest to explore and learn all things, we require that all things be mysterious and unexplorable" (317). And so, while the very ending is exultant, even triumphant—"There is more day to dawn. The sun is but a morning star" (333)—we must also note that it envisions a fulfillment that is still prospective. The book deliberately makes itself preliminary to a completion that can be accomplished—if at all—only by its reader.

Not that one should expect anything else from such a paradoxical and conflicted book. *Walden* is thickly allusive, sometimes pedantic, and yet tries to wean us from a dependence on books, including itself. It attempts to create for itself a permanent structure, yet one that is open and responsive to the unexpected spontaneities of life. It tries to fashion a new language by burrowing into the most antiquarian roots of the one we have already. It gives us a sense of future possibilities by appealing to some of our most regressive fantasies. It embeds itself in the Western philosophical and religious tradition only to undermine its basic assumptions. And it engages all these complexities in the context of a plea for simplicity, simplicity. Its final wisdom is that there is no final wisdom, that all truths are mediate, volatile, and that what can be conveyed to a reader is not a teaching but an intensity of response to life.

Notes and References

1. The Two Americas and Transcendentalism

1. Richard Poirier, *A World Elsewhere: The Place of Style in American Literature* (New York: Oxford University Press, 1966).

2. James Freeman Clarke, Ralph Waldo Emerson, and W. H. Channing, eds., *Memoirs of Margaret Fuller Ossoli* (Boston: Phillips, Sampson, 1852), 2:14.

3. Nathaniel Hawthorne, *Tales and Sketches* (New York: Library of America, 1982), 817.

4. Ralph Waldo Emerson, *Essays and Lectures* (New York: Library of America, 1983), 198–99; hereafter cited in text.

2. The Importance of the Work

1. Don Henley and Dave Marsh, eds., *Heaven Is under Our Feet: A Book for Walden Woods* (Stamford, Ct.: Longmeadow Press, 1991).

3. Composition and Reception

1. Edward Connery Lathem, ed., *Interviews with Robert Frost* (New York: Holt, Rinehart and Winston, 1966), 143.

2. J. Lyndon Shanley, *The Making of "Walden"; with the Text of the First Version* (Chicago: University of Chicago Press, 1957).

3. Ronald Clapper, "The Development of *Walden*: A Genetic Text," Ph.D. diss., University of California at Los Angeles, 1967.

4. Robert Sattelmeyer, "The Remaking of *Walden*," in *Writing the American Classics*, ed. James Barbour and Tom Quirk (Chapel Hill: University

of North Carolina Press, 1990), 60.

5. Bradley P. Dean and Gary Scharnhorst, "The Contemporary Reception of *Walden*," in *Studies in the American Renaissance, 1990*, ed. Joel Myerson (Charlottesville: University Press of Virginia, 1990), 293.

6. Henry Miller, *Tropic of Cancer* (New York: Grove Press, 1961).

7. Robert Louis Stevenson, "Henry David Thoreau: His Character and Opinions," in *The Recognition of Henry David Thoreau*, ed. Wendell Glick (Ann Arbor: University of Michigan Press, 1969), 82.

8. F. O. Matthiessen, *American Renaissance: Art and Expression in the Age of Emerson and Whitman* (New York: Oxford University Press, 1941); hereafter cited in text.

9. R. W. B. Lewis, *The American Adam: Innocence, Tragedy, and Tradition in the Nineteenth Century* (Chicago: University of Chicago Press, 1955).

10. Leo Marx, *The Machine in the Garden: Technology and the Pastoral Ideal in America* (New York: Oxford University Press, 1964); hereafter cited in text.

11. Walter Harding, *The Days of Henry Thoreau: A Biography* (1965; enlarged and corrected edition, New York: Dover, 1982).

12. William Howarth, *The Book of Concord: Thoreau's Life as a Writer* (New York: Viking, 1982).

13. Sharon Cameron, *Writing Nature: Henry Thoreau's Journal* (New York: Oxford University Press, 1985).

14. Robert D. Richardson, Jr., *Henry David Thoreau: A Life of the Mind* (Berkeley: University of California Press, 1986).

15. Robert Sattelmeyer, *Thoreau's Reading: A Study in Intellectual History with Bibliographical Catalogue* (Princeton, N.J.: Princeton University Press, 1988).

16. Charles R. Anderson, *The Magic Circle of "Walden"* (New York: Holt, Rinehart and Winston, 1968), 18; hereafter cited in text.

17. Stanley Cavell, *The Senses of "Walden"* (New York: Viking, 1972), 66. Viking Compass paper edition, 1974; hereafter cited in text.

18. Cornel West, *The American Evasion of Philosophy: A Genealogy of Pragmatism* (Madison: University of Wisconsin Press, 1989).

19. The most obvious and prominent case is Leon Edel, *Henry D. Thoreau* (Minneapolis: University of Minnesota Press, 1970).

20. H. Daniel Peck, *Thoreau's Morning Work: Memory and Perception in "A Week on the Concord and Merrimack Rivers," the Journal, and "Walden"* (New Haven: Yale University Press, 1990).

21. Henry Golemba, *Thoreau's Wild Rhetoric* (New York: New York University Press, 1990).

22. Frederick Garber, *Thoreau's Fable of Inscribing* (Princeton, N.J.: Princeton University Press, 1991).

5. Structurings: The Form of Flow

1. James Russell Lowell, *My Study Windows* (Boston: Houghton Mifflin, 1871), 200.

2. Odell Shepard, ed., *The Heart of Thoreau's Journals* (Boston: Houghton Mifflin, 1927), vi–vii.

3. R. P. Adams, "Romanticism and the American Renaissance," *American Literature* 23 (1952): 424.

4. Sherman Paul, *The Shores of America: Thoreau's Inward Exploration* (Urbana: University of Illinois Press, 1958), 323–53.

5. Lauriat Lane, Jr., "On the Organic Structure of *Walden*," *College English* 21 (1960): 197–98.

6. Jonathan Culler, "Prolegomena to a Theory of Reading," in *The Reader in the Text: Essays on Audience and Interpretation*, ed. Susan R. Suleiman and Inge Crosman (Princeton, N.J.: Princeton University Press, 1980), 47.

7. Martin Bickman, "Flawed Words and Stubborn Sounds: Another Look at Structure and Meaning in *Walden*," *Southern Humanities Review* 8 (1974): 153–62.

8. James McIntosh, *Thoreau as Romantic Naturalist: His Shifting Stance toward Nature* (Ithaca, N.Y.: Cornell University Press, 1974).

9. Walter Benn Michaels, "*Walden*'s False Bottoms," *Glyph* 1 (1977): 133–49.

10. Ralph Waldo Emerson, *Poems* (Boston: Houghton Mifflin, 1904), 42.

11. Henry D. Thoreau, *A Week on the Concord and Merrimack Rivers*, ed. Carl F. Hovde, William L. Howarth, and Elizabeth Hall Witherell (Princeton, N.J.: Princeton University Press, 1980), 343; hereafter cited in text as *A Week*.

12. Henry Adams, *Novels; "Mont Saint Michel"; "The Education"* (New York: Library of America, 1983), 728; hereafter cited in text.

13. Henry D. Thoreau, *Early Essays and Miscellanies* (Princeton, N.J.: Princeton University Press, 1975), 3.

14. Henry D. Thoreau, *The Natural History Essays*, ed. Robert Sattelmeyer (Salt Lake City: Peregrine Smith, 1980), 2; hereafter cited in text as *Natural*.

15. A. E. Elmore, "Symmetry Out of Season: The Form of *Walden*," *South Atlantic Bulletin* 37 (1972): 18–24.

6. Languages: Root Meanings

1. Ralph Waldo Emerson, in *Journals and Miscellaneous Notebooks of Ralph Waldo Emerson, Volume VIII: 1841–43*, ed. William Gilman and J. E. Parsons (Cambridge, Mass.: Harvard University Press, 1970), 96.

2. Herman Laurence Eisenlohr, "The Development of Thoreau's Prose," Ph.D. diss., University of Pennsylvania, 1966, 131–32.

3. *The Correspondence of Henry David Thoreau*, ed. Walter Harding and Carl Bode (New York: New York University Press, 1958), 125; hereafter cited in text as *Correspondence*.

4. *The Complete Poems of Emily Dickinson*, ed. Thomas H. Johnson (Boston: Little, Brown, 1960), 257.

7. Paradise (To Be) Regained

1. Edward Waldo Emerson, *Henry Thoreau as Remembered by a Young Friend* (Boston: Houghton Mifflin, 1917), viii.

2. *"Poems, in Two Volumes," and Other Poems, 1800–1807*, ed. Jared Curtis (Ithaca, N.Y.: Cornell University Press, 1983), 273.

3. Allen B. Hovey, *The Hidden Thoreau* (Beirut: Catholic Press, 1966).

4. Northrop Frye, "The Drunken Boat: The Revolutionary Element in Romanticism," in *Romanticism Reconsidered: Selected Papers from the English Institute* (New York: Columbia University Press, 1963), 17–18.

5. Walter Harding, ed., *The Variorum "Walden"* (New York: Twayne, 1962), 270–72.

6. J. Hillis Miller, *Poets of Reality: Six Twentieth-Century Writers* (Cambridge, Mass.: Harvard University Press, 1965), 7–8.

7. Lewis Leary, "Henry David Thoreau," in *Eight American Authors: A Review of the Research and Criticism*, rev. ed., ed. James Woodress (New York: Norton, 1971), 132.

8. Philosophy: Heaven Can Wait

1. John Dewey, *Characters and Events* (New York: Holt, Rinehart and Winston, 1929), 2:843.

2. Letter from John Dewey to Walter Harding, *Thoreau Society Bulletin* 30 (1950): 1.

3. Ernest Hemingway, *The Sun Also Rises* (New York: Charles Scribner's Sons, 1926), 148.

4. Joan Burbick, *Thoreau's Alternative History: Changing Perspectives*

on Nature, Culture, and Language (Philadelphia: University of Pennsylvania Press, 1987), 59–82.

5. Daniel J. Boorstin, *The Americans: The Colonial Experience* (New York: Random House, 1958), 159.

6. Richard H. Brodhead, *Hawthorne, Melville, and the Novel* (Chicago: University of Chicago Press, 1976), 153.

Selected Bibliography

Primary Works

Editions of *Walden*

Walden; or, Life in the Woods. Boston: Ticknor & Fields, 1854. First edition, and only one for which Thoreau read proof, although he made 16 further corrections in his own published copy. After this edition the subtitle was omitted, honoring a late request by Thoreau.

Harding, Walter, ed. *The Variorum "Walden."* New York: Twayne, 1962. Paper edition, New York: Washington Square Press, 1963. Uses first edition as copytext and presents Thoreau's later corrections only in the notes. Contains generous annotations that distill much of the scholarship up to its time. Numerical superscript notes in text itself are distracting; the first chapter, for example, has 229 of them.

Sayre, Robert F., ed. *A Week on the Concord and Merrimack Rivers; Walden; The Main Woods; Cape Cod.* New York: Library of America, 1985. Well edited, readable texts, including maps, notes, chronology.

Shanley, J. Lyndon, ed. *Walden.* Princeton, N.J.: Princeton University Press, 1971. First volume published in Princeton Edition of the Writings. Although its accuracy as a text has been questioned, it has become the standard edition to which criticism, including the present book, is keyed. The same text and page numbers are also in Princeton's *The Illustrated "Walden"* and in its smaller-format paper edition with a foreword by Joyce Carol Oates.

Stern, Philip Van Doren, ed. *The Annotated "Walden."* New York: Clarkson N. Potter, 1970. Photographic reproduction of first edition, with helpful background essays, notes, and illustrations.

Thomas, Owen, ed. *"Walden" and "Civil Disobedience."* New York: Norton,

128

1962. An accurate text, using the first edition, but incorporating Thoreau's later corrections. A helpful selection of background and critical essays.

Ziff, Larzer, ed. *"Walden": A Writer's Edition*. New York: Holt, Rinehart and Winston, 1961. Insightful comments and questions on each chapter.

Other Writings by Thoreau

Early Essays and Miscellanies. Princeton, N.J.: Princeton University Press, 1975.

A Week on the Concord and Merrimack Rivers. Boston: James Munroe, 1849. Best modern edition, Princeton, N.J.: Princeton University Press, 1980.

The Maine Woods. Boston: Ticknor & Fields, 1864. Princeton, N.J.: Princeton University Press, 1972.

Cape Cod. Boston: Ticknor & Fields, 1864. Princeton, N.J.: Princeton University Press, 1988.

The Natural History Essays. Edited by Robert Sattelmeyer. Salt Lake City: Peregrine Smith, 1980.

The Correspondence of Henry David Thoreau. Edited by Walter Harding and Carl Bode. New York: New York University Press, 1958.

The Journal of Henry Thoreau. Edited by Bradford Torrey and Francis H. Allen. 14 volumes. Boston: Houghton Mifflin, 1906.

Journal 1: 1837–1844. Edited by Elizabeth Hall Witherell, William L. Howarth, Robert Sattelmeyer, and Thomas Blanding. Princeton, N.J.: Princeton University Press, 1981.

Journal 2: 1842–1848. Edited by Robert Sattelmeyer. Princeton, N.J.: Princeton University Press, 1984.

Journal 3: 1848–1851. Edited by Robert Sattelmeyer, Mark R. Patterson, William Rossi. Princeton, N.J.: Princeton University Press, 1990.

Secondary Works

Biographies

Channing, William Ellery. *Thoreau: The Poet-Naturalist*. Boston: Roberts Brothers, 1873. Written by Thoreau's walking partner on many excursions, this anecdotal and diffuse memoir is the first full-length biography.

Harding, Walter. *The Days of Henry Thoreau: A Biography*. 1965. Enlarged and corrected edition, New York: Dover, 1982. Still considered the authoritative biography.

————, ed. *Thoreau as Seen by His Contemporaries*. New York: Holt, Rinehart and Winston, 1960. Revised edition, New York: Dover, 1989. Useful and thorough collection of first-hand accounts, culled not only from published sources but also from diaries and letters.

Lebeaux, Richard. *Young Man Thoreau*. Amherst: University of Massachusetts Press, 1977. Based on Harding's data, this is an Eriksonian interpretation of Thoreau's identity crisis.

————. *Thoreau's Seasons*. Amherst: University of Massachusetts Press, 1984. A continuation of the *Young Man Thoreau*, this volume relies heavily on recent psychological theories about adult life cycles.

Richardson, Robert D. *Henry David Thoreau: A Life of the Mind*. Berkeley: University of California Press, 1986. In this detailed and readable intellectual biography, the author has accomplished the formidable task of reading everything Thoreau is known to have read.

Critical Studies: Books

Adams, Stephen, and Donald Ross, Jr. *Revising Mythologies: The Composition of Thoreau's Major Works*. Charlottesville: University Press of Virginia, 1988. Although thesis that *Walden* was radically reshaped by Thoreau's "discovery" of romanticism is strained, this book contains a wealth of computer-collated data on its subject.

Anderson, Charles. *The Magic Circle of "Walden."* New York: Holt, Rinehart and Winston, 1968. Longest and richest formalist reading.

Boudreau, Gordon V. *The Roots of "Walden" and the Tree of Life*. Nashville: Vanderbilt University Press, 1990. An informed but often heavy-handed reading; strongest point is analysis of Thoreau's wordplay.

Bridgman, Richard. *Dark Thoreau*. Lincoln: University of Nebraska Press, 1982. An antidote to hagiography, this study dwells on what it sees as Thoreau's weakness as a writer and as a person.

Buell, Lawrence. *Literary Transcendentalism: Style and Vision in the American Renaissance*. Ithaca, N.Y.: Cornell University Press, 1973. Particularly helpful on genres and modes.

Burbick, Joan. *Thoreau's Alternative History: Changing Perspectives on Nature, Culture, and Language*. Philadelphia: University of Pennsylvania Press, 1987. Informed New Historicist reading of entire career; especially helpful on dynamics of perception in *Journal*.

Cavell, Stanley. *In Quest of the Ordinary: Lines of Skepticism and Romanticism*. Chicago: University of Chicago Press, 1988. Views Emerson and

Thoreau as forming a crucial but repressed tradition in American philosophy; important extension and recasting of ideas in previous *The Senses of Walden*.

———. *The Senses of "Walden."* New York: Viking Press, 1972. Viking Compass paper edition, 1974. Expanded edition (with two essays on Emerson), San Francisco: North Point Press, 1981. Although dense and difficult to read itself, this is a vital and stimulating interpretation.

Friesen, Victor Carl. *The Spirit of the Huckleberry: Sensuousness in Henry Thoreau*. Edmonton, Canada: University of Alberta Press, 1984. Repetitive, but a valuable counterbalance to views of Thoreau as too ascetic or spiritual.

Garber, Frederick. *Thoreau's Fable of Inscribing*. Princeton, N.J.: Princeton University Press, 1991. Traces Thoreau's obsession with trying to be at home in the world through the act of inscribing himself in books, houses, tracks.

———. *Thoreau's Redemptive Imagination*. New York: New York University Press, 1977. This earlier book is clearer than *Thoreau's Fable of Inscribing* and is particularly insightful on the dialectics in Thoreau's thought and his relation to romantic movements in England and America.

Glick, Wendell, ed. *The Recognition of Henry David Thoreau: Selected Criticism since 1848*. Ann Arbor: University of Michigan Press, 1969. Helpful for tracing the shifts in Thoreau's reputation, but now superseded by Myerson.

Golemba, Henry. *Thoreau's Wild Rhetoric*. New York: New York University Press, 1990. Analyzes Thoreau's conflicting tendencies to present a clear argument but also to create a language distrustful of definite positions.

Harding, Walter, ed. *Henry David Thoreau: A Profile*. New York: Hill and Wang, 1971. Reprints several key but hard to find pieces, such as those by Daniel Ricketson, Charles Ives, and Raymond D. Gozzi.

——— and Michael Meyer. *The New Thoreau Handbook*. New York: New York University Press, 1980. An updating of Harding's previous *A Thoreau Handbook* (1959), the volume contains excellent reviews of scholarship up to date of publication.

Henley, Don, and Dave Marsh, eds. *Heaven is under our Feet: A Book for Walden Woods*. Stamford, Connecticut: Longmeadow Press, 1991. Celebrities, politicians, and writers offer brief narratives, usually with environmental themes, on the significance of Thoreau for them; proceeds go to conserving Walden Woods from development.

Howarth, William. *The Book of Concord: Thoreau's Life as a Writer*. New York: Viking, 1982. As one of its editors, the author uses the *Journal* as a lens to view the entire writing career.

Johnson, William C., Jr. *What Thoreau Said: "Walden" and the Unsayable*.

Moscow, Idaho: University of Idaho Press, 1991. Despite its promising paradoxical title, this reading based on Coleridge's notion of bipolarity contains few fresh or clear ideas.

Lane, Lauriat, Jr., ed. *Approaches to Walden*. Belmont, California: Wadsworth Publishing Company, 1961. Constructed as a casebook for undergraduate "research," this collection reprints both literary appreciations by writers such as William Butler Yeats and E. B. White along with critical analyses.

Marx, Leo. *The Machine in the Garden: Technology and the Pastoral Ideal in America*. New York: Oxford University Press, 1964. View of American classics as "complex pastorals" works particularly well with *Walden*.

McIntosh, James. *Thoreau as Romantic Naturalist: His Shifting Stance toward Nature*. Ithaca, N.Y.: Cornell University Press, 1974. Intelligent reading of Thoreau's inconsistencies and relation of work to Goethe's.

Matthiessen, F. O. *American Renaissance: Art and Expression in the Age of Emerson and Whitman*. New York: Oxford University Press, 1941. Crucial chapter on Thoreau set down lines of further criticism for many years.

Myerson, Joel. *Critical Essays on Henry David Thoreau's "Walden."* Boston: G. K. Hall & Co., 1988. Its collection of early reviews now needs to be supplemented by Dean and Scharnhorst, but contains several crucial modern articles, some of them original with this volume.

Peck, H. Daniel. *Thoreau's Morning Work: Memory and Perception in "A Week on the Concord and Merrimack Rivers," the "Journal," and "Walden."* New Haven: Yale University Press, 1990. Views these three works through Thoreau's strategies of at once preserving and transcending the temporal.

Poirier, Richard. *A World Elsewhere: The Place of Style in American Literature*. New York: Oxford University Press, 1966. Perceptive reading of Thoreau's verbal pyrotechnics as well as helpful conceptual framework for American literature.

Paul, Sherman. *The Shores of America: Thoreau's Inward Exploration*. Urbana: University of Illinois Press, 1958. Detailed and influential reading of all Thoreau's writings.

———, ed. *Thoreau: A Collection of Critical Essays*. Englewood Cliffs, N.J.: Prentice Hall, 1962. Reprints what had become the standard essays up to date of publication.

Ruland, Richard, ed. *Twentieth Century Interpretations of "Walden": A Collection of Critical Essays*. Englewood Cliffs, New Jersey: Prentice-Hall, 1968. Another collection of standard critical essays.

Sattelmeyer, Robert. *Thoreau's Reading: A Study in Intellectual History with Bibliographical Catalogue*. Princeton, N.J.: Princeton University Press, 1988. Excellent introductory essay on Thoreau's shifting intellectual interests.

Schneider, Richard J. *Henry David Thoreau*. Boston: Twayne, 1987. Accurate and intelligent introduction to life and works.

Selected Bibliography

Shanley, J. Lyndon. *The Making of "Walden"; with the Text of the First Version*. Chicago: University of Chicago Press, 1957. Discovery and interpretation of the seven manuscript versions.

Steele, Jeffrey. *The Representation of the Self in the American Renaissance*. Chapel Hill: University of North Carolina Press, 1987. Extends Joel Porte's notion of Thoreau turning away from Emersonian idealism towards the body and the natural world; effective use of Heidegger and modern psychologists.

Tuerk, Richard. *Central Still: Circle and Sphere in Thoreau's Prose*. The Hague: Mouton, 1975. A theme-and-image study.

Critical Studies: Articles

Adams, R. P. "Romanticism and the American Renaissance." *American Literature* 23 (1952): 419–32. *Walden* as an example of the shift between the image of the universe as a static mechanism to a more organic one, valuing instinct, freedom, change over reason, order, and permanence.

Adamson, Joseph. "The Trials of Thoreau." *ESQ* 36 (1990): 137–72. Emphasizes aspects of "trying" in forensic, scientific, and especially rhetorical senses.

Baker, Larry. " 'The Ponds' as Linkage." *Thoreau Journal Quarterly* 13 (1981): 21–27. Both Walden Pond and *Walden* are metaphors for the linking process itself, as suggested by an analysis of the four sections of this central chapter.

Boone, Joseph Allen. "Delving and Diving for Truth: Breaking through to Bottom in Thoreau's *Walden*." *ESQ* 27 (1981): 135–46. Collates references to probing downwards into earth and water as metaphors for seeking reality.

Borck, Jim Springer, and Herbert B. Rothchild, Jr. "Meditative Discoveries in Thoreau's 'The Pond in Winter.' " *Texas Studies in Language and Literature* 20 (1978): 93–106. Counterpointing of trade and contemplation in close reading of key chapter.

Boudreau, Gordon V. "H. D. Thoreau, William Gilpin, and the Metaphysical Ground of the Picturesque." *American Literature* 45 (1973): 357–69. Thoreau was both influenced by and ultimately rejected the vision of major English theorist of the picturesque.

Broderick, John C. "American Reviews of Thoreau's Posthumous Books, 1863–1866: Checklist and Analysis." *University of Texas Studies in English* 34 (1955): 125–39. Discovers a surprising amount of favorable interest.

———. "The Movement of Thoreau's Prose." *American Literature* 33 (1961): 133–42. An influential study that relates circular movement of excursions to patterns in the writing.

Buell, Lawrence. "American Pastoral Ideology Reappraised." *American Literary History* 1 (1989): 1–29. Sophisticated reexamination of American pastoral forms, using *Walden* as a central example.

———. "The Thoreauvian Pilgrimage: The Structure of an American Cult." *American Literature* 61 (1989): 175–99. Incisive analysis of cultural attitudes.

Dean, Bradley P., and Gary Scharnhorst. "The Contemporary Reception of 'Walden.' " *Studies in the American Renaissance* (1990): 293–328. Reprints 56 notices and reviews from the 1850s, supplementing the 37 already reprinted in Myerson's *Critical Essays on Henry D. Thoreau's "Walden."*

Devery, Edward S., Jr. "A Re-examination of Thoreau's 'Walden.' " *The Quarterly Review of Biology* 17 (1942): 1–11. In studying both Walden Pond and *Walden* from the point of view of limnology, the author concludes that Thoreau was an accurate and skilled observer.

Dillman, Richard. "The Psychological Rhetoric of *Walden.*" *ESQ* 25 (1979): 79–91. Examines Thoreau's use of the newer rhetorical theories he was exposed to at Harvard.

Elmore, A. E. "Symmetry out of Season: The Form of *Walden.*" *South Atlantic Bulletin* 37 (1972): 18–24. Explores further how cycle of seasons relates to structure.

Galligan, Edward L. "The Comedian at Walden Pond." *South Atlantic Quarterly* 69 (1970): 20–37. *Walden*'s relations to traditional genre of comedy and to tall tale.

Gould, Timothy. "Reading On: *Walden*'s Labors of Succession." *Thoreau Quarterly* 16 (1984): 119–36. A close reading of "Reading," especially in relation to the views of Emerson and Stanley Cavell.

Gross, Robert A. "Culture and Cultivation: Agriculture and Society in Thoreau's Concord." *Journal of American History* 69 (1982): 42–61. Excellent background on the changes in farming brought on by the railroad and by social factors.

———. "Much Instruction from Little Reading: Books and Libraries in Thoreau's Concord." *Proceedings of the American Antiquarian Society* 97 (1987): 129–88.

Gura, Philip F. "Henry Thoreau and the Wisdom of Words." *New England Quarterly* 52 (1979): 38–54. Uses Thoreau's understanding of Charles Kraitsir's language theories to unlock cruxes in the passage on thawing clay.

Harding, Anthony John. "Thoreau and the Adequacy of Homer." *Studies in Romanticism* 20 (1981): 317–32. Beginning with Thoreau's college essay on Greek poetry, goes on to discuss relation between classics and present writing and living, especially in "Reading" chapter.

Hocks, Richard A. "Thoreau, Coleridge, and Barfield: Reflections on the

Imagination and the Law of Polarity." *Centennial Review* 17 (1973): 175–98. Maintains that through Coleridge's sense of complementary opposites, Thoreau sees wilderness and civilization in ways that are mutually defining.

Lane, Lauriat, Jr. "On the Organic Structure of *Walden.*" *College English* 21 (1960): 195–202. Discusses five different structuring principles that somehow all work together.

Lorch, Fred W. "Thoreau and the Organic Principle in Poetry." *PMLA* 53 (1938): 286–302. Thoreau's critique of Carlyle, as influenced by the Germans and Coleridge.

Lyon, Melvin E. "Walden Pond as Symbol." *PMLA* 82 (1967): 289–300. Argues that pond represents aspects of Thoreau's self and encompasses other image patterns.

McConahay, Mary Davidson. " 'Into the Bladelike Arms of God': The Quest for Meaning through Symbolic Language in Thoreau and Annie Dillard." *Denver Quarterly* 20 (1985): 103–16. Links *Walden* to *Pilgrim at Tinker Creek* through genre, through the use of a body of water as central symbol, and through a stance toward symbolism itself.

McElrath, Joseph R., Jr. "Practical Editions: Henry D. Thoreau's *Walden.*" *Proof* 4 (1975): 175–82. Careful and informed discussion of the accuracy of texts available for college courses.

Moldenhauer, Joseph J. "Images of Circularity in Thoreau's Prose." *Texas Studies in Literature and Language* 1 (1959): 245–63. Relates theme and style convincingly.

O'Brien, Geoffrey. "Thoreau's Book of Life." *New York Review of Books* 33 (1987): 46–51. Ostensibly a review of three recent books, this article contributes toward a reading of Thoreau's life and work.

Orth, Michael. "The Prose Style of Henry David Thoreau." *Language and Style* 7 (1974): 36–52. Detailed analysis of the passage on thawing clay to show a distinctive style in American Renaissance writers, one focusing on symbolism and organicism.

Sattelmeyer, Robert. "The Remaking of *Walden.*" 53–78. In *Writing the American Classics*, edited by James Barbour and Tom Quirk, Chapel Hill: University of North Carolina Press, 1990. Most recent and most convincing discussion of composition. Traces movement from a stress on social reform and outward change to deeper psychological and meditative concerns, towards a more complex and sophisticated vision.

Schwaber, Paul. "Thoreau's Development in *Walden.*" *Criticism* 5 (1963): 64–77. Book as record not only of life at pond but of nine years of composition.

Skwire, David. "A Check List of Wordplays in *Walden.*" *American Literature* 31 (1959): 282–89. Helpful but incomplete.

West, Michael. "Scatology and Eschatology: The Heroic Dimensions of Thoreau's Wordplay." *PMLA* 89 (1974): 1043–64. Relates use of puns to Thoreau's tuberculosis as understood by the medicine of the day. Provoking correlations between different areas of Thoreau's life.

Woodson, Thomas. "The Two Beginnings of *Walden*: A Distinction of Styles." *ELH* 35 (1968): 440–73. Proposes that the two beginnings, the first journal entry made at the pond and the opening of Thoreau's first lecture about his life there, are paradigmatic of the two poles of style, the private and the social.

Index

Index

The Author

Martin Bickman, a graduate of Amherst College, Harvard Graduate School of Education, and the University of Pennsylvania, is currently associate professor of English at the University of Colorado. He is the author of *American Romantic Psychology* and editor of the Modern Language Association volume *Approaches to Teaching Melville's "Moby-Dick."* His articles have appeared in *Poe Studies, College Literature, Science-Fiction Studies, ESQ,* and other journals. He has received the Boulder Faculty Assembly Teaching Award, the Faculty Teaching Fellowship, and, most recently, a lifetime appointment as President's Teaching Scholar. An educational activist, he works with both public and private schools at various levels and is now writing a book on the history and philosophy of student-centered learning in America. He lives in Boulder with his wife, Louise, and their children, Sarah and Jed.

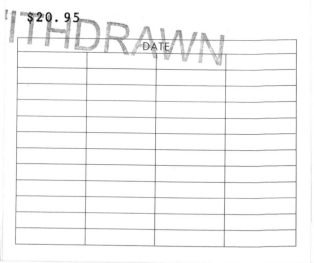